Living Leadership

Living Leadership
Biblical Leadership
Speaks to Our Day

Kenneth F. Hall, Editor

The Board of Christian Education
of the Church of God
and
Warner Press, Inc.
Anderson, Indiana

Published by
Warner Press, Inc.
Anderson, Indiana

About Bible Translations
  Except where indicated otherwise, quotations from the Bible are from the Holy Bible, New International Version, Copyright, 1984, by International Bible Society and are used by permission. Passages marked TEV are from Today's English Version, those marked RSV are from the Revised Standard Version, those marked JB are from the Jerusalem Bible, and are used by permission of the publishers. Passages marked KJV are from the King James Version. Occasional use of biblical material involves personal paraphrases by the writers, and these are indicated by the context or by special footnote.

Arlo F. Newell, Editor in Chief
Dan Harman, Book Editor
Cover by David Liverett

Contents

Donald Addison Courtney 1929-1986

Dedicated with love
and admiration to
Donald Addison Courtney

Introduction

A Matter of Leadership
by Kenneth F. Hall

The conference leader stood up, turned to her group, and asked: "What is the biggest problem you have in the work of your church these days?"

"Finding the right people to do all the work we have in our congregation," said one.

"Just finding enough people to get things done is what we face," said another.

"And then we need to help people develop their skills and grow as they serve," chimed in another.

"We have trouble helping our people relate to each other in an effective team." This comment came from a pastor.

"We don't seem to know what it is we are really about and how to get to where we should be," put in a young man.

The responses of these conference members are typical of what happens in church workshop after workshop, conference after conference. Add in other concerns about the way people plan and administer their programs or ministries, and include concerns about recognizing and responding to calls from the Lord and gifts that are to be found in congregations.

When we look at the common denominator in all these concerns, we are seeing issues related to leadership. Here is a concern, a set of issues that seems common to local churches and church service agencies, large and small, in all parts of North America and around the world. Leadership has been a part of church concern for many years. It is here and now. And it is urgent.

Why This Book?

Into this scene comes this book, yet another volume concerned with leadership. It does not come offering panaceas but with the hope of speaking here and there to people who can make a difference in the church's leadership picture. It is going to make some assumptions. One is that the potential for leadership is great and that something can be done in the development of leaders other than to assume that leaders are just born, not made.

The book, in its dedication to the memory of Donald A. Courtney, is going to make some of the same assumptions that he made about leadership, although among the many friends of Don who contribute to this book there are some differences of emphasis on what leadership is all about. Yet it is going to pick up on the emphases that Don made in his ministry of Christian education about the centrality of the leadership concern.

What Is Leadership?

The assumption is sometimes made that leadership is simply an impressive word to cover over what is really a question of power and of getting one's own way by dominating other people and getting them to do what we want them to do whether they like it or not. That had better not be what leadership is really about. People sometimes assumed that leadership is a magical matter, a kind of mantle that some people inherit through the accident of birth or by being in the right place at the right time in order to be named to a designated place of power and influence known as leadership. That had better not be what leadership is really about.

In considering what leadership means, of course, we do have to take into account the part that influence plays. Healthy leadership involves the capacity to influence others in the particular group one is in toward a worthy central purpose and with concern for the well-being of the group members involved. There are good and bad uses of influence just as there is good and bad leadership. There are worthy and unworthy purposes. There are both benefits and troubles for the groups involved.

Implications for Leadership

Such a definition is loaded with immediate implications that are important to the writers of this book. Leadership as influence assumes immediately that a group is involved. There is the leader doing the influencing of followers. There are followers being influenced. They are together, and that means a group is involved. Hence leadership immediately involves us in all the dynamics that go with group life and participation with others.

The definition suggests that there are common goals, perhaps a central purpose that the leader is seeking to influence others to move toward. Sometimes such purposes are clear-cut, at other times vague and almost nonexistent. At any rate an assumption is being made here that leadership relates to goal or purpose setting, clarification, and implementation.

A third aspect of this definition involves us in the nature of the group and its well-being or health. A leader is bound up closely with this part of group life. Some leaders are highly oriented toward the accomplishment of the purpose for which the group exists, and in that sense the leader becomes task-oriented. At other times or with other leaders they become highly focused on the way the group gets along, what happens to the individuals in it, and how well the group relates. Such leaders become maintenance oriented.

The church in the past hundred years has become increasingly conscious of leadership as a need, as an issue, as a consideration that determines much about the way the church operates. While we do not find the term isolated as such in the Bible, clearly the Bible has much to say about leadership through the kinds of persons it introduces to us, through the events that spring out of leadership skills or weaknesses, and through its teachings across long biblical eras about how we respond to our gifts, our callings, and our relationships with other people.

Because the Bible is so basic to what the church is all about and because it has so much to say with implications for leadership, we have chosen to structure this book with its message about leadership today on a study of selected leaders in the Bible. Except for seeking out a variety of leaders across Old and New Testament, we do not claim comprehensiveness or even complete balance in teaching about leadership here. We do feel that our somewhat-random look at the stories connected with the leaders we have chosen gives us ample opportunity to consider pertinent issues for leadership in the church today.

This book is written to leaders, and that includes a surprisingly large group of church people. Again using the definition offered, we find that most Christians are already leaders of some sort in their church. Whenever they are influencing a group, even if but for a moment, they are in that situation and for that moment a leader. We are moving well beyond the few who are in widely recognized designated positions of leadership in the church. We are speaking to a circle well beyond those who have been specifically, often dramatically, called to fill a certain spot in God's kingdom. We are going beyond those apparently born with all the gifts and tools and skills to be leaders. The book is based on the premise that through increasing skills, developing as persons, and strengthening personal relationships with our Lord, we can all be more effective in whatever roles of leadership we find ourselves from time to time and situation to situation. The church, with its priesthood of all believers, is going to be stronger, and we as leaders are going to be stronger as we grasp the moments, the changing opportunities, the particular callings open to us to lead in the church.

Central Issues in Leadership

In understanding leadership as the exertion of influence toward a purpose or goals within a group context, we are opening up several central issues or concerns.

1. One issue has to do with power. By what authority will the leader lead? Where are the roots of authority out of which the leader exerts influence? In the tradition of the Hebrew people, we note that situations seem to move along at their best when God is allowed to be the authority. Moses and Deborah led best when they served as spokespersons for God. The Hebrew people were at their best at those times when they most sensitively followed God rather than when they were under a king who took authority unto himself. Solomon saw some great results come to his reign and in his own power. But all that started with Solomon being very much aware that his strength must necessarily come from the Lord. Whenever David or Solomon or any king moved from being a channel of God's authority to his own, trouble started. Almost invariably anything like a kingship that resulted in a human autocracy—and all the kingships did—the king himself and his people would soon be in trouble. On the other side of that issue we find in Jesus himself and in people like Barnabas a leadership that brought to bear the authority of God with a free response and a concern for ownership by the people themselves. That

was a most significant leadership approach to power.

Through the calling of God, through leaders seeking to follow the will of God, through recognition of the gifts that God has given his people, we have seen leaders taking up their responsibilities with a helpful orientation to the ultimate power of God.

2. A second issue has to do with defining the task or tasks the group will seek together to accomplish. What is the leader's role in presenting purposes and goals, helping to clarify them, and keeping the group oriented to its task? Does the leader simply lift up the mission and march ahead of the followers toward the goal? Will the mission or the cluster of goals move in a more global or more individual and local direction? How will progress be measured? How will ownership of the mission and commitment to it be widely obtained across the group?

All through the Old Testament we get a changing picture regarding the clarity of vision and purpose. Occasionally the gray clouds drift apart and we view the blue sky and a clear mission of God. When this vision is clear to the eyes of the leaders and when they communicate clearly with the people, the people move ahead with victory and confidence. Under any circumstance, our progress toward goals needs to be measured and the steps along the way be noted and understood. Some questions emerge: How will goals be measured? How will ownership of the task before the group be widely obtained? Or, is it even necessary to obtain wide ownership?

3. A third issue emerges from the definition that leadership involves both influencing a group toward the accomplishment of set tasks and the maintenance of a healthy and coherent group life. What should be the priorities here? Is the accomplishment of the task always or sometimes first and foremost? Is the maintenance of group life always an essential? What kind of balance and weighing do we give to this? Some leaders are more task-oriented, others more maintenance oriented, and in group life and work the emphases shift.

4. In relation to these issues, a fourth umbrella issue emerges for us. Just how shall we approach the study of leadership and the education of persons in relationship to it? The application for us is principally to pastoral roles and to related laity roles. The following section examines some of these approaches.

Approaches to an Understanding of Leadership

a) *Looking at Leadership Traits*—Perhaps the most traditional approach to thinking about leadership has been to reflect on the characteristics of great women and men we think of as leaders or to compile adjectives to describe the ideal persons we would present as leaders. We can do that going through the Bible and through history and drawing from individuals those traits we think of positively as helpful to leadership and those we think have had negative effects. Those leaders that seem to us to be the greatest then seem to offer to us qualities that we should seek to emulate in our own leadership roles and foster in other potential leaders.

Telling the stories of great leaders, modeling our lives after the great heroes of the faith—these are some ways we can teach leadership following this approach. In such studies we can see how God related to these leaders. We can see the qualities portrayed that had good results and those that led to mistakes and failures. In the modeling process, people almost unconsciously take on the characteristics they admire. Thus an admired pastor may see a number of young people go forth to study for the ministry and then turn out to be pastors in the same style as he or she. It is notable how often the call of God or the gifts that come to a person bear some resemblance to the call of God or the gifts that are a part of the ministry characteristics of the influential pastor, teacher, parent, friend, or church hero.

A list of characteristics or traits of a good leader is a helpful and traditional tool in the study of leadership. Such an approach, however, has been added to or superseded by other approaches in our time.

b) *Considering Leadership Styles*—A second approach, not unrelated to the above, is to come at leadership through an exploration of appropriate styles. Here there is a tendency to cluster some of the traits just listed and put them in relational terms under rubrics related to the exercise of power and authority. Almost always the current leadership material does this with some expansion on or variation of the following terms:

(1) Autocratic leadership. This may be subdivided into such titles as tyrant, benevolent dictator, or godfather. The category generally refers to a highly authoritarian, usually coercive style.

(2) *Laissez-faire* leadership. Here the leader sits back and lets events take their course without much interference. The result can be directionless, wandering, and seemingly purposeless. Occasionally this is seen as a developmental stage almost everyone passes through momentarily on the way from an autocratic to a more democratic format.

(3) Democratic leadership. This is the more consultative, participative leadership style. It sometimes includes such additional categories as the collegial, which moves beyond rule by the majority to a consensus approach among equals.

Other clusterings of basic leadership styles speak of how one leads in relation to authority and have fairly typical effects on the followers involved. Sometimes the degree of task-orientation compared with group-member orientation is suggested. Sometimes these are seen in developmental stages of both leaders and followers. For example, a dependent, law-and-order person with a strong desire to please would welcome and respond positively to a benevolent-dictator style of leadership much more readily than to a democratic leader.

c) *Positional Leadership*—Obviously some people lead by position. The elected president of the United States has certain constitutional requirements to meet. A queen of England inherits her position and exerts at least a degree of authority simply by the fact that she is queen of the realm. A factory supervisor is employed to fulfill a certain leadership function as suggested by a job description and perhaps limited by a union contract. A pastor occupies a positional leadership slot.

Of course such positions may be filled in strong or weak ways. The person in the position may by nature be more or less suitable for the position, and circumstances may be supportive or not.

Some observers in this area would hope for a more relational way of describing positional leadership. Hence we get suggestions of understanding some leadership callings within the church and elsewhere as ministries. Some would use the term *shepherd* in church leadership. Here also we encounter servant leadership terminology that both fulfills the spirit of Christ's ministry and carries implications of leadership style and for hierarchical organizational structures and lines of responsibility.

In any study of leadership that focuses on positions then, terms like *administration* come up, and with them a theology of the church comes into focus that sees it more as organic than organizational.

How do these positions and the underlying philosophies of leadership relate to church organism in the body of Christ? Considerable attention is given in the church to organizational charts and lines of responsibility.

With this would normally go a rather positional kind of approach to the study of leadership. With this it is important to consider credentials, job descriptions, administration guidelines, and the like.

d) *Situational and Distributive Approaches to Leadership*—A number of leadership approaches associated with names like Bale, Fiedler, Herzog, and Blanchard and with terms like Theories Y and Z have been evolving in recent years even though they describe leadership processes that go back to the earliest of times.

The general assumption of the distributive theories is that leadership functions are shared by members of a group, that leadership does not concentrate only in the designated areas of position, special call, and an accumulation of certain traits. Whoever at the moment has a contribution to make that influences the group in the direction of its goals or in goal setting or in contributing to the health of the group is for that moment a leader. So leadership is distributed widely, and leadership concerns in the church, therefore, involve everyone who shares in the life of the church and its groups.

A second element here is that leadership situations vary so much from time to time and place to place and depend so much on the tasks involved and the kinds of people involved that no single and permanent prescribed approach to leadership can fulfill the needs of changing situations.

An illustration of this from Herzog and Blanchard is that, depending on the task involved and the readiness of the group, the leadership function might move from telling to selling to participating to delegating. Any one of these might be right or wrong for the situation, depending on what it is. We certainly find a wide range of leadership styles in the Bible depending on the situation. We find a wide range of leadership traits and leadership roles.

Fostering Leadership Skills

The study of leadership is not an exact science. But some principles related to it evolve from biblical narrative, Jesus' teachings, the experience of history. These principles and values about leadership can come to be encouraged through the educational ministry of the church.

Each of the approaches mentioned here (and others that might be added) provides clues for how leadership may be encouraged along lines that seem most desirable. It is probably the distributive-situational concept that has some of the most direct implications for the church's leadership in education ministry. It says that all people have some leadership contributions to make and therefore are in need of our facilitating them. It says that there are collections of group and task related skills connected with leadership, and since they are skills they can indeed be taught. For some writers these fall under the heading of

● Instrumental skills (developing specific abilities for getting certain tasks accomplished)
● Interpersonal skills (developing specific abilities for relating to persons and fostering the health and cohesiveness of the group involved)
● Imaginal skills (developing the abilities to think and work creatively and originally in solving problems and leading groups beyond current horizons)
● And especially the culminating systems skills (in which one develops on a rather mature level a combination of abilities involving the other three categories that allow one to know how to influence wisely and well all the parts of whatever system one is a part of)

This view, more than the others, says there is something to be done about leadership as we educate women and men for the leadership service of the church, and that we have a fairly wide potential clientele to deal with. It also says that matters are perhaps more complex than we sometimes have assumed. There are several kinds of leadership approaches to prepare for and to use wisely. There are also developmental differentials to be aware of. That involves teachers or leaders in understanding the developmental levels of themselves, their students, and the groups to be served and in knowing the nature of the varying leadership tasks to be undertaken. Leadership involves no static situation with simple answers but a very complex set of dynamics.

It is not simply a matter of being born to lead or having a peculiar set of qualifications for leadership or being in the right place at the right time to be elected or appointed or brought by inheritance into a leadership spot.

For the Christian there remain as well the central dynamics of being gifted and called by Christ and relating meaningfully to the Christian fellowship.

So here is some of the vocabulary connected with leadership studies in our day and here are some of the approaches. Here is some of the context for leadership development as a part of the process of education for ministry.

Chapter 1
Joseph: Why a Great Leader?

A. Joseph

by Arlene S. Hall

What kind of future would you predict for a teen-ager who was self-centered, cocky, irritating, assertive, a tattle-tale, and spoiled? Not very promising, is it? But that describes young Joseph exactly. The eleventh of twelve sons, he was his father's favorite. While his brothers wore grubbies for their work of tending sheep, Joseph wore a long, colorful, flowing robe that set him apart in any crowd, a robe most often worn by nobility or the wealthy.

Favored Son

While his brothers toiled endlessly at herding sheep, Joseph stayed at home with his adoring father. How he lorded it over his eleven brothers! He bragged, "I dreamed about you. Your eleven sheaves fell down in homage before mine—and that isn't all. In another dream the sun, moon, and eleven stars bowed down to me, too."

No wonder his brothers hated him. What they would do to him if they ever caught him alone! Then came their opportunity. Jacob sent Joseph to Shechem to see how his older sons were getting along. When they saw that dazzling robe coming down the trail, they plotted to kill him and throw his body into a cistern. They would say a wild animal had eaten him. Their hatred seethed, fermented, and became the urge to kill. Reuben intervened, and Joseph found himself in a deep, dark pit, listening to the furious threats of his brothers.

Reuben went off with his flocks, and still the brothers discussed murder. At that very moment a caravan happened along, headed for Egypt. On the spur of the moment they sold Joseph as a slave. The brothers danced with joy, for their troubles were over. Never again would they have to worry about their uppity brother! Perhaps they laughed and taunted him as he was being led away, "Where are your dreams now, Joseph?"

A Slave and a Foreigner

Imagine his despair. From favored son in a large, wealthy family to slave among foreigners speaking a different language, far from home. Brokenhearted, desperate, alone, forsaken, hopeless. What had he done to make his brothers so angry? He worked at answering that question.

And he was alone—except for God. Did he remember his father telling about going far away from home alone and being assured of God's help? Surely this was the time that God and Joseph became good friends. Joseph was strengthened in his inner being.

Joseph—young, strong, and good looking—would be a prize slave. He was purchased by Potiphar, Pharaoh's captain of the guard. Joseph didn't have time to feel sorry for himself, for he worked long, demanding hours. He put all his mental and physical energies into the job at hand. And he succeeded very well! Eventually he became second to Potiphar. "The Lord was with Joseph."

Potiphar's wife was especially attracted to handsome, young Joseph and she wanted him to become her lover. Even in his loneliness Joseph resisted her invitations. She could wait to catch him in a moment of weakness. Day after day she urged him, never giving up. He reviewed the situation in his mind time after time. He was trapped. How do you complain to your boss about his wife?

Then came that day when the other servants were gone. She grabbed his coat and laughed, "See, Joseph, I've got you at last." But Joseph slipped out of his coat and fled.

A Prisoner

That's how he landed in prison. Potiphar's wife, furious at being rejected by a mere slave, created quite a scene and reversed the story, accusing Joseph of making advances.

A man has a lot of time to think in prison. If those thoughts are bitter, he destroys himself. Again Joseph must have turned to God. He would do his best even in this very difficult, ugly, oppressive place. Although treated like a criminal, he did not act like one. He was willing to face himself and his situation, to make the best of his present opportunities.

Opportunities in prison? Joseph thought so. He was a model prisoner—willing, cooperative, and helpful. The jailer gave him more and more responsibilities until finally he was in charge of all the prisoners. "The Lord was with him; and whatever he did, the Lord made it to prosper."

Here in prison he met Pharaoh's butler and baker. One morning he noticed the two were upset. They had been troubled by strange dreams and were anxious to find out what the dreams meant. Joseph told them, and their dreams were fulfilled just as he said. As the butler left to return to Pharaoh, Joseph implored him, "Remember me to Pharaoh."

But the butler forgot, and Joseph was betrayed again. Instead of giving up and wallowing in self-pity, he turned to God and found renewing strength and patience.

Two years later the butler remembered. Pharaoh had

two disturbing dreams that no one could interpret. Joseph was sent for in prison. Modestly he told the ruler, "God will give Pharaoh a favorable answer."

The dream revealed Egypt's future—seven years of bountiful harvests followed by seven years of famine. Pharaoh was stunned. What would he do about this gigantic problem? Joseph suggested Pharaoh appoint an overseer who would gather in one-fifth of the abundant harvests for use during the years of famine.

"Great idea!" Pharaoh said, "and you are just the man for the job. I can tell God is with you."

Awesome Responsibility

This time Joseph's trauma was very different. How does one handle the awesome responsibilities of a huge promotion along with all the emotions of going from prison to palace? The signet ring, fine linen clothing, a chain of gold, a new name—these became the symbols of the high office. Never did Joseph question the God-given interpretation of Pharaoh's dream.

At last thirty-year-old Joseph was free to marry. Two sons were born to Joseph and Asenath. Their names reflect a little of the pain and sorrow Joseph had endured through the years: Manasseh, meaning God made me forget my hardship in my father's house, and Ephraim, meaning God has caused me to be fruitful in the land of my affliction. At last he had a home and family of his own. In their love, memories of the past began to heal and the future looked promising.

The seven prosperous years found Joseph traveling throughout Egypt, overseeing the reception and storage of grain. The famine followed, not just in Egypt but in all the countries round about, even in Joseph's homeland.

A Needy Family

About a year later Jacob and his sons had used up all

their food supplies. The old patriarch had heard there was grain for sale in Egypt. Impatiently he asked his ten sons, "Why do you sit here looking at one another? Go to Egypt at once."

This bunch of sheepherders stood out in sophisticated Egypt. Joseph recognized them at once. What kind of men had they become? In his own way he would find out. Through an interpreter he spoke to them, harshly accusing, "You are spies!" The brothers began to explain to this high Egyptian official who they were and why they had come. Then Joseph threatened, "You shall not go until your youngest brother comes here." With that the ten were put in jail.

How Joseph longed to see Benjamin, his youngest brother! On the third day he proposed, "Leave one brother here in prison while the rest of you return home with provisions. Then bring your youngest brother back."

In prison the brothers had plenty of time to think. They remembered their sin against Joseph and against their father. Those heavy, buried feelings were uppermost in their minds. Reuben reminded, "Didn't I tell you not to harm him?" Joseph was overwhelmed. He turned away so they could not see his tears.

As they prepared to return home, Simeon was tied up and returned to prison. Joseph ordered his servants, "Fill the bags with grain and put their money on top. Give them whatever provisions they need for their journey."

On the way home they opened one sack to prepare a meal. There on top was the money they had paid. Terrified, they asked, "What is God doing to us?"

Back home they gave a full account to Jacob, including the order, "Bring your youngest brother." Jacob would not listen to such a ridiculous demand. Hadn't he already lost Joseph, and now Simeon?

Their terror multiplied when all the sacks of grain were opened, revealing their money on top. Now they were sure they would never go back to Egypt.

Time passed. The brothers and their families grew

hungry again. Without food they would die. In spite of their fears they must take Benjamin and return to Egypt. They remembered the Egyptian overseer's stern order, "You shall not see my face unless Benjamin is with you."

"Why did you tell them about Benjamin?" Jacob complained sorrowfully.

Again the brothers explained patiently, "He questioned us over and over about ourselves and our kin. He asked if our father was still alive."

Judah bargained, "Send the lad with me. I will be responsible for him." He gave his own family as a pledge of Benjamin's safety.

With heavy heart Jacob sent gifts, double the money, and Benjamin. As they traveled across the miles, each man's fear grew.

On their arrival in Egypt a feast was prepared for them at Joseph's house. Their fear intensified. What kind of trick was this? Would he make them his slaves forever? Joseph said, "Peace to you, fear not." But their fear remained.

The brothers explained to the steward that they had found money in their sacks, but they had brought double the amount to settle the account. The steward assured them, "You have nothing to worry about." Tension eased a bit when Simeon was allowed to join them.

At noon Joseph arrived. They bowed down to him in fear and respect. "How is your father?" he asked, "and is this your youngest brother?" Overcome with emotion Joseph ran from the room. When his tears had stopped and his emotions were under control, he returned.

"Let the food be served," he announced. Joseph was seated at a table by himself, but the brothers were seated together at the next table by age. How could the Egyptian know that?

Food was brought from Joseph's table, but Benjamin's helpings were five times larger than his brothers.' Their tension dissolved in the joy of the occasion. Surely everything was all right this time.

When the brothers were ready to return home, Joseph secretly told his steward, "Fill the sacks with grain and place the money on top. Put the silver cup in Benjamin's sack."

With lighter hearts the brothers set off for home. Before long they were overtaken by Joseph's men. Angrily they accused, "Why have you done this dastardly thing to our master? Why have you stolen his silver cup?"

The brothers looked at one another in disbelief. None of them would do such a thing. They felt so certain that they promised, "If you find Joseph's cup in one of our sacks, you can kill the person the sack belongs to and the rest of us will be your slaves."

The Egyptians agreed. Every man lowered his sack to the ground. From the oldest to the youngest they were searched. That's when the worst happened. The cup was in Benjamin's sack. In complete desperation they tore their clothes and returned to the city.

At Joseph's house they fell on their faces before him. Judah said, "We are your slaves."

"No," Joseph replied, "only the person who had the cup."

Judah pleaded, "Oh, sir, please have mercy on our old father. He did not want our brother Benjamin to make this trip. He has already lost his favorite son Joseph. Now with Benjamin gone too, the pain would kill him."

One by one the brothers said, "Please have pity on our old father. He will die when he hears this news."

Judah came up with a new proposal. "Let me stay in his place."

A Family Reunion

Joseph could contain himself no longer. Sending his employees out of the room, he began to sob, "I am Joseph, your brother. Is my father really still alive?"

The brothers were awe-struck. How could this be? If

he were really Joseph, what would he do to get even? They shuddered with fear.

But Joseph said, "Come closer. Don't be upset or angry. God has sent me before you to preserve life, to save you during this famine. It was not you who sent me here but God. He made me a father to Pharaoh."

At first the brothers could not believe what they were hearing. Gradually hope and faith overcame their fear. Through their tears the brothers embraced each other. But Joseph could not bring himself to part with Benjamin. At last he said, "Hurry back to my father and bring all your families. You will live here in Goshen. I will see that you have plenty to eat during these five remaining years of famine." He paused for breath and added, "Hurry and bring my father."

A large caravan of carriages and wagons rumbled out of the city to get Jacob, all their families, and their possessions. This time they took wonderful news: Joseph was alive!

No one could describe the reunion of Joseph and his father Jacob—love and tears and smiles and promises and thankfulness. Jacob said, "I didn't think I would ever see you again, but God has let me see not only you but your children, too." The extended families enjoyed seventeen years together before Jacob died. How good God had been to each of them.

B. Why a Great Leader?

by Arlene S. Hall

Rich Spiritual Resources

Joseph knew his strength, wisdom, and insight came from God. He relied on God to direct him. When God made himself known, Joseph did not question but carried out that direction as fully as possible. He was focused Godward as a life stance. Alone in a foreign country, he found God his sole support. Later as his work and his relationships developed, God was still given priority.

All the credit for Joseph's accomplishments was given to God. Sometimes successful leaders are tempted to take credit for themselves. Joseph never succumbed to that temptation.

On the journey to Egypt and during those years in prison, Joseph had time to meditate, to be open toward God, to reflect on the events of his life with spiritual insight. He responded to whatever happened as a gift from God. No wonder he could say of the tragic events, "But God meant it for good." So his task became finding out what that good was, rather than railing against the painful situation itself.

His deep inner resources were evident when Potiphar's wife pursued him. Even when no one would know, he could not relent, for God would know. Such an act would go against the highest and best he knew. It would make him a stranger to himself. His inner resources held him steady.

Spiritual resources that hold a person steady both in times of painful trauma and in the aura of sweet success are wonderfully real. This was not a faith of mere words or rituals. It was a faith of action, affirmative responses, deep trust, and commitment.

These spiritual resources enabled him to forgive—even those who had hurt him the most. His brothers, Potiphar's wife, and the butler were persons who had done their best to make him live his life in the pits. But Joseph's sights were set much higher.

Later this same inner strength made it possible for him to step confidently into a primary leadership role in behalf of all Egypt. He didn't say, "But I've never done anything of this magnitude before." Nor did he add, "This task is so large that I am overwhelmed." Nor did he plead, "I've never had any experience in leading a whole country." Joseph was willing to be God's person even in a gigantic undertaking.

This inner directedness made him intuitive in his lifestyle. He trusted the present moment. He did his best in the task at hand and left the future to God.

Good Relater

Except for his early years at home, Joseph related well to people. He seemed to know how to work with his employers, his co-workers, and his employees. He must have understood people. Wherever he was, Joseph inspired confidence in the persons around him. Potiphar entrusted everything to this young man. The jailor put most prison responsibilities into his hands, and Pharaoh made him second in power in all Egypt. How often our attitude toward people determines their attitude toward us.

Joseph was sensitive toward people. He could see the butler and the baker had had a sleepless night, and he wanted to help. They found him an easy person in whom to confide.

Probably the Egyptian people resisted taxes as much as we do today. Seven years of having to give the government one fifth of your harvest would not have created great joy. Nor would the seven years of rationing that followed. But Joseph drew out the people's cooperation.

To relate well to persons means there will be times of confrontation. Not one to back down in a tough situation, Joseph as an adult confronted his brothers in love and forgiveness. His forgiving spirit saved him from being poisoned by resentment toward those who had wronged him. He did not nurture resentment. Instead he treated persons with generosity.

Potiphar, the jailor, Pharaoh, and even his brothers would have said that loyalty was one of Joseph's traits. That trait put him in good stead again and again. It enabled him to be an effective leader.

Good Work Habits

Work was not something Joseph had learned to do at home as a favorite son, but he took to it readily. Quite possibly he found a freedom in work, an avenue for self-expression, or just a wonderful way to forget his troubles.

Joseph's diligence as a good, dependable, imaginative worker earned him promotions. He had a way of climbing the ladder of success by hard work and ambition. From the very start he did the common task uncommonly well. He disciplined himself to be able to produce good results.

When he saw a task that needed doing, he did it willingly without being told. He enjoyed responsibility.

Part of Joseph's work was physical, and part of it was mental—planning, executing those plans, evaluating, correcting. Whatever the assignment, he gave it his best.

Trustworthy

Joseph had developed a lifelong habit of being honest and fair in all his dealings. He spoke truthfully and kept his promises. Employers could trust him to do his best, to keep his word, to look out for their interests. He was not a young man out to succeed in the quickest way possible. Nor did he use people to gain his own advantage.

Sincerity characterized his dealing with people. He was a man of integrity.

No wonder Joseph had a reputation for being trust-worthy. Persons around him recognized this trait and gave him more and more responsibility. To the best of his ability he was faithful to each task.

Patient and Persevering

How patient he was! Willingly he waited for God's appointed time with alert eyes, ears, and heart. Nor did he merely cool his heels and mark time. While he set himself to whatever needed doing, he waited expect-antly. That ability held him steady during the years of watching and waiting for God's goodness to unfold. Some of us can wait a few minutes, but for a leader to wait for years requires traits that few of us know.

A Positive Attitude

When in the midst of adversity, he did not give up in despair. He hung on to the difficulty until it became an advantage. Too often we picture in our minds the condi-tions we think God will create to further God's work. If those conditions do not develop, there may be anxiety, worry, even despair. But God's plans and our plans are very different. Joseph trusted in God supremely—in both God's timing and methods. That made it possible for him to be flexible and adaptable to whatever happened.

Joseph was so cooperative in finding the best in the present circumstances that the hard knocks only served to kick him forward. Sold by his brothers into slavery in a foreign country, falsely accused by Potiphar's wife, years in prison when he had done nothing wrong—these were circumstances that would have paralyzed some of us, kept us depressed. Joseph used each of these harsh experiences as opportunities for learning, growth, train-ing. He used each one as an opportunity to develop new skills, to relate to new people, to find quiet times for deepening his trust in God.

Courageous

Through his difficult life experiences, Joseph developed the ability to stand alone. Bit by bit he grew in courage. Some of us admire that trait and would like to have it if courage could be ordered by mail or telephone or be delivered tomorrow, but we do not want the hard struggles that produce courage and bravery.

As a youth of seventeen Joseph had never been far from home. Suddenly he was on his own in a foreign country. His first job, a promising one, almost destroyed him when he was falsely accused by a designing woman. Courage, integrity, and faith saw him through.

How amazing was Joseph's courage in interpreting and carrying out a bold design to secure the future for a whole nation! There was no doubting or wishy-washyness here. Joseph believed God's plan even when it was completely out of his realm of experience. He proceeded with boldness, confident that it would be just as God had ordained.

Responsible for His Own Actions

When things went awry, Joseph did not look for a scapegoat and blame circumstances or others. Nor did he hold grudges. Although he was deeply injured by his brothers' action, nothing in the story indicates that he blamed them.

Thrown into prison through no fault of his own and left there years longer than seemed necessary, he did not give in to self-pity and feel sorry for himself. He did not alibi or make excuses. He was not only responsible for his own actions but also for the attitude he took toward his circumstances.

When the situation looked desperate, Joseph never

13

gave up. Instead he started all over again, making the most of what he had. He never complained or criticized, for he trusted God, the persons around him, and the future. His expectations were always hopeful.

Nor was Joseph a wild-eyed optimist, but a realist who concentrated on the positive. He did not allow his spirit to be sunk by disaster, for he controlled his thoughts and his outlook. He knew how to live in the present moment without putting too much stock in past successes or being sidetracked by his hopes for the future.

Persons with a positive attitude are usually confident. Over and over again Joseph trusted God, himself, other persons, and the situation. That's a winning combination for ultimate success.

Good Administrator

Whether in Potiphar's household, in prison, or in the palace, Joseph was a gifted administrator, overseeing one project after another. He was a problem-solver. Making decisions, even tough ones, was not difficult for him. Not only could he plan, he could put those plans into action.

Evidently he could delegate responsibilities to others, for it would have taken the cooperation of many people to create a national food distribution plan. Good record keeping would have been a necessity.

Whatever the situation, Joseph always had the larger picture in mind. That made delays, interruptions, problems, and details easier to deal with.

Servant Leader

Doing menial chores does not necessarily indicate a servant leader. Instead a servant leader is one who invests himself or herself in enabling others, in helping them be and do their best. The servant leader qualities of Joseph became obvious when he was in prison. These qualities and his abilities to use them increased as he grew older.

As Pharaoh's overseer, Joseph enabled a whole nation to survive in years of bountiful harvest and in years of famine. Thus Joseph was truly a savior of a nation. He based his life not on his own interests but on the needs of the people around him. He fulfilled God's calling.

Visionary

Joseph had great ability to see beyond today. He dreamed about possibilities, about how life could be in the future. This trait began in childhood with his dreams about his brothers. As he grew older, he gained perspective. No longer did he use his dreams to lord it over other persons.

Handling the present is easier when there are dreams for the future. Joseph's imagination became an important tool. Using this gift to picture the best possible scenario, his dreams were harnessed to discipline as a way of transforming them into reality. Willingly he placed himself at God's disposal to enable God's dreams to come true. His vision from God meant life for an entire people.

Chapter 2
Moses and Aaron:
A Look at Leadership

A. Moses and Aaron

by Donald R. Brumfield

The Commission (Exodus 3:1-10)

"I will go over and see this strange sight."
—Exodus 3:3

The working shepherd sees the bush is aflame, but it does not burn up. He climbs the ridge to investigate. The voice of "him who dwelt in the burning bush" (Deut. 33:16) calls the shepherd by name, "Moses, Moses." Addressed with respect and on a person-to-person level, Moses responds quickly, "I am here." "Stay where you are. Take off your shoes; you are standing on holy ground" (3:5). A spirit of dread seizes Moses. He now becomes very aware of the Holy-other difference between his humanness and God who appears in power and transcendent glory. Solemnly, Moses bares his feet. Then the voice speaks again: "I am the God of your father, the God [Shield] of Abraham, and God [Fear] of Isaac, and the God [Strength] of Jacob." Moses, now overwhelmed by the presence of the God who dwells among humankind, hides his face. He is afraid to look at God (3:16).

There are cultural reasons why Moses was overwhelmed by the self-revealing of Yahweh. In Egyptian

17

worship, the gods never appeared outside the temples. The deities remained in the holy place where alone they were to be encountered on special days only. All matters pertaining to the divine were handled by priestly intermediaries. As for the Israelites, the centuries of direct exposure to the Egyptian deities and practices along with the harshness of their slave labor caused them to despair of deliverance. Except for a few families of faith, Israel remembered no more the words of Joseph, the father who brought them into Egypt: "But God will surely come to your aid and take you up out of this land to the land he promised on oath to Abraham, Isaac, and Joseph" (Gen. 50:24).

Moses recalls the reason for his own exile in this desert country. Some forty years ago, out of passion for the promise and compassion for his people, he acted impulsively. He presumed that fellow Israelites would understand deliverance by his hand (Acts 7:25). But the killing of the Egyptian brought him rejection and alienation from both the courts of Pharaoh and the community of Israel. He was considered to be contemptuous and ungrateful by Pharaoh. He was judged presumptuous and irrational by the community of Israel. Condemned, rejected, and disillusioned, he fled into the land of Midian. Now, here in this sparse country, through the help of his father-in-law Jethro, his self-confidence was slowly being restored. As for his faith, he was still searching for the God who appeared unto his fathers but who for centuries has been silent, unresponsive to the cries and groanings of his brothers and sisters in bondage.

Then the Lord said, "I have indeed seen the misery of my people in Egypt. I have heard them crying out because of their slave drivers, and am concerned about their suffering (Exodus 3:7) . . . I have come down to rescue them from the hand of the Egyptians (3:8) . . . and I have seen the way the Egyptians are oppressing them" (3:9). The revelation to Moses is that of a God who acts not above history but in and through history (Davis 71).

God uses the powers and events of kings of the nations to work God's will and purpose.

God was active in the policies of Pharaoh and Joseph to preserve the house of Jacob in time of famine by bringing them into Egypt, and God permitted the various kings of Egypt to enslave the children of Israel until the sins of the Canaanites were fulfilled. So now God will contest the power of this Pharaoh who refuses to let God's firstborn, Israel, go up to their Promised Land. It is time (kairos) for God to deliver his people with his "outstretched arm." But to do this, God's action needs the help of persons living in history (Knight 21). God's call to Moses is specific: "Go. I am sending you to Pharaoh to bring my people, the Israelites out of Egypt" (3:10).

Self-assessment (Exodus 3:11-13; 4:1-16)

The righteous call of God exposed the sinfulness and humanity of Moses. It brought to the surface of his being all the feeling of self-condemnation, rejection, and inadequacy. He recoils from the request of God to join him in pain of going back into the Egyptian situation. Moses offers God the first of five excuses: "Who am I, that I should go to Pharaoh and bring the Israelites out of Egypt?" (3:11). The thought of facing the arrogant King and the sneers of his people filled him with dread. He felt himself too inferior and worthless to fulfill so demanding a task.

God responds in a direct and understanding way. "I will be with you. And this will be the sign to you that it is I who have sent you . . . you shall worship God on this mountain (3:12). The promise of God to Moses is that the sending and the sign are one. The medium is the message (Knight 23). "True," God seems to be saying, "sending you into Egypt and rescuing your people out from under the nose of Pharaoh is quite preposterous. But I will accomplish it with the power of my strong, right hand. Proclaim the Word and it shall come to pass. You will stand on this very mountain with my people and worship me. It will become a fact of history" (Knight 22).

But Moses was concerned more with the difficult demands of the task rather than the sufficiency of God. He raises another objection: "Suppose I go to the Israelites and say to them, 'The God of your fathers has sent me to you,' and they ask me, 'What is his name?' Then what shall I tell them?" (3:13). Moses was deeply concerned by his lack of authority to represent God before the Israelites. Usually, a document with a seal was offered to signify the bearer as the spokesperson for the king. "In whose name," Moses asked, "can I tell them I come?"

God said to Moses, "I AM WHO I AM. This is what you are to say to the Israelites: I AM [the one who is] has sent me to you" (3:14). If we may paraphrase the scriptures here, God is saying, "I am the same God who cared for your fathers and who now cares for you. I am here, now, active in the present with you as I was with your fathers in the past and will be with your children in the future. They will believe you, and you and the elders will go to Pharaoh and tell him to let my people go."

Moses raises a third objection to the commission of God: "What if they do not believe me or listen to me and say, 'The Lord did not appear to you'?" (4:1) Recalling the superstition and magical arts that flourished in Egyptian culture, Moses is certain that he will be asked to authenticate his commission of God by some sign. He fears the people will discount God's appearance to him in the burning bush as merely an illusion on his part. Thus, he requests of God a powerful sign that would excel the secret crafts of the magicians proving thereby that he is God's sent one.

God accommodates Moses by giving him three signs. First, he would be able to turn his staff into a serpent and back to a staff again. Second, he would cause his hand to turn leprous and back to whole again. Third, water taken from the Nile River when poured upon the ground would turn to blood (4:1-8). Speechless now perhaps, but he had not always been so! Else how could he have risen to courtly position and privilege as the son of Pharaoh's daughter? Or, how could he, as a general of Pharaoh's army, rally his troops to victory in the Ethiopian campaign? Tradition states that Moses was a man of power in words and deeds (Acts 7:22). Or is Moses feeling out of touch after forty years of absence from the courtly and political life in Egypt? Whatever he was thinking, God feels great sympathy for this felt deficiency in Moses and assures him by saying, "Who gave man his mouth? . . . Is it not I, the Lord? Now go; I will help you speak and will teach you what to say" (4:11-12).

Moses still has not grasped that he is to be merely the servant of the Word and not the Word itself. Once again he objects to God's choice of himself as the one to send. "O Lord, please send someone else to do it" (4:13). This refusal brings a sharp rebuke from God, for this answer goes beyond feelings of disability to disobedience. Moses continues acting out of his sinful, defeated self-centeredness rather than in the creative power of God's self-revealing presence of I AM, I WILL BE [COME] WITH YOU. God refuses to dismiss Moses as the chosen believer. He alters his plan by adding Aaron as the spokesperson for Moses: "What about your brother, Aaron the Levite? I know he can speak well. He is already on his way to meet you, his heart will be glad when he sees you" (4:14).

The Team (Exodus 4:15-17; 27-31)

Aaron meets Moses at the mountain of God and kisses him: "Shalom, my long lost brother." We can picture their conversation going like this.

"How did you know where to find me?" Moses asks as he returns the embrace.

"There were many rumors regarding your fate. We

also heard an occasional word by way of the Bedouins at the sheep market who told of an Egyptian living in the house of Jethro the Midianite. We wondered if that could be you; we hoped it would be. But recently an angel of the Lord appeared to me in a dream and told me, 'Go into the desert to meet Moses' (4:27). So I am here. Tell me, what is the urgency of this meeting?"

Moses goes directly to the point. "It is the appointed time for the deliverance of our people from their bondage to the Egyptians as promised in the oath given by God to our fathers Abraham, Isaac, and Jacob. This same God has appeared to me in a new name, I AM THE ONE WHO WILL BE [COME] WITH YOU, and he has commissioned me to be the one to carry his Word to Israel and to Pharaoh."

Aaron inquires, "How do I fit into this mission?"

"When I raised objections of not being one who could speak persuasively and argumentatively, God permitted you to become my spokesperson," Moses answers.

"Am I to speak for you in the same way you speak for God?" questions Aaron.

"That is the way God put it," says Moses. "You shall speak to him and put words in his mouth. . . . He will speak to the people for you, and it will be as if he were your mouth and as if you were God to him" (4:15, 16).

"This is an awesome responsibility," Aaron says softly.

"Yes," Moses agrees. "But God promised that he would help both of us to speak and teach us what to do" (4:15). One other fact needs to be clarified: The older is serving the younger. "How do you feel about that?"

"The thought did occur to me, but then who am I to argue with God's choice of the leader? It is apparent from the manner in which God has preserved your life that his hand has been heavy upon you. No, the difference in years will not interfere with my loyalty to you and to God," affirms Aaron. "But now, tell me more about the miraculous signs."

"As I told you, there are three. These are more than

the conjured tricks of the local magicians used to deceive the people," states Moses. "Those sorcerers give the impression that the gods can be manipulated into doing things for the people. But these signs God has given are to be performed while declaring the Word of God, thus impressing the hearer to accept the reality that God is doing a great work through this messenger for the benefit of God's people."

"And what is God declaring through these signs?" asks Aaron.

"I will tell you what insights I received from them," Moses exclaims. "By casting the staff on the ground and it turning into a live serpent, I discovered that in obeying God's command to pick it up by the tail, frightened though I was, I could grip evil itself by the tail. And by trusting God I am doing what God does, that is, making use of evil to bring about a new creative act of God."

"In this instance, it was the serpent becoming a good staff again," exclaims Aaron. "Now what of the second sign? What did you learn?"

"The hand becoming leprous and then back to being whole again," explains Moses, "taught me that God is the one who brings affliction and judgment and then makes whole again, restoring life. He is the one who takes life and gives life. He it is who is the Lord of life and death."

"And the third sign?" asks Aaron.

"Taking water from the Nile and pouring it upon the ground where it turns into blood," states Moses, "presents a view of what God will do to Egypt by way of the plagues: disease, social upheaval, and finally, the death of the firstborn. It will be a time of judgment upon the gods of Egypt, Pharaoh, and his people for their cruel enslavement of Israel for these hundreds of years."

"Perhaps Pharaoh will permit our people to go out of Egypt, once he hears the request of God to let his people go," says Aaron.

"No, for God knows the heart of the king of Egypt,"

counters Moses. He will not let our people go unless compelled by a mighty hand. But then, even Pharaoh's stubbornness of heart will work to Israel's advantage" (see 3:19-22).

"I begin to see the plan," answers Aaron. "So, then, it's God, you, and me against Pharaoh?"

"Yes, but don't forget my staff," Moses adds. "It is to be used in performing miraculous signs" (4:17).

The Task (4:29-31; 5:1-15, 21)

Aaron assembles all the elders of the Israelites and introduces Moses. He relates to them everything that God said to Moses. "He also performed [three] signs before the people, and they believed. And when they heard that the Lord was concerned about them and had seen their misery, they bowed down and worshiped" (4:29-31).

Having received the blessings of the elders, and having been officially ordained as the representatives of the "nation of Israel," the stage was set for the encounters with the king of Egypt. The first meeting most likely took place somewhere near the Delta region. If an early date of the Exodus is accepted, this king would be Amenhotep II. Those accepting a later date suggest Rameses II as the Pharaoh who is encountered (Davis 80). Aaron speaks for Moses, "This is what the Lord, the God of Israel, says: 'Let my people go' " (5:1).

Pharaoh inquires, "Who is the Lord, that I should obey him and let Israel go? I do not know the Lord and I will not let Israel go" (5:2).

Thus, the contest between the God of Egypt and the God of Israel commences. And it is only after twelve dramatic encounters that the winner emerges. Israel began their Exodus from Rameses to Succoth in the month of Abib (April) about 1450 BC.

Moses

Abraham, Moses, and David are revered as leaders of the Jewish faith. Abraham is their father, but Moses is deliverer and lawgiver. Moses, which means "drawn out" (Egyptian) or "to draw out" (Hebrew), was born to Amram, his father, and Jochebed, his mother. Both were of the tribe of Levi (Exodus 6:20). Living in an alien environment that was steeped in idolatry and opposed to all that God had revealed to their ancestors, Moses' parents remained true to the God of Israel. When Moses was born, they by faith believed that God would preserve his life for "he was a beautiful child" (Exod. 2:2). All the biblical accounts and the *Antiquities* of Joseph record that Moses was outstanding in physical assets, intellectual accomplishments, leadership ability, and strength of character (integrity). Such personal traits contributed to his advancement in the educational, political, and military systems of Egypt. He, no doubt, was a bright, good looking, energetic, take-charge, motivational kind of leader—and for forty years he had the world at his feet. Life was an unbroken series of successes. Moses may have felt that there was nothing that he couldn't do.

But Moses was to learn that privilege, power, passion, and impulse make for a volatile combination in people-to-people relationships (2:11-15). In Exodus and Numbers one reads encounter after encounter in which Moses, acting under God's direction, initiates creative action that brings deliverance, plenty, and harmony. But, that same Moses, acting impulsively and overriding commands, results in alienation, rebellion, judgment, and death. We have, as it were, a personal diary of a man who records his successes and failures in his growing relationship with the God Who Will Become with You as he fulfills his commission as the anointed deliverer of Israel.

25

Aaron

He is the older brother of Moses by three years. He is selected to assist Moses by the permissive will of God rather than the prescriptive will. Aaron is permitted to join Moses when God becomes impatient with Moses, who was still struggling within his low self-image as an unskilled speaker. So Aaron is delegated to accompany Moses and assist him in communicating with the elders of Israel and with Pharaoh. His task is to speak the actual mind of the leader; he is to be the "talking chief" (Knight 52).

It is a temporary arrangement—only until Moses regains his self-confidence and faith to speak and act for God. And as the account shows, Aaron is the spokesperson up and through the first three plagues (7:14—8:19), but then by the fourth plague, Moses is speaking to Pharaoh and performing the miracles himself (8:20—11:4). Moses becomes the predominant leader at this point (Getz 63).

The complicity of Aaron in the people's sin of making a golden calf and the jealousy exhibited when he joined Miriam in contesting Moses' right to be the sole speaker for God, reveal personality traits that nullify a leader's influence (Num. 12:1-6). To his credit, however, he was tenderhearted. He was quick to repent and ask for mercy for Miriam, his sister. Aaron proved to be better suited as a delegated follower than as the primary leader. In this position of leadership, he served in the priestly office.

Pharaoh

"Who is the Lord, that I should obey him?" (Exodus 5:2). Pharaoh's refusal to recognize the name of God or a request in that name, was a decision well within his right as the ruler of Egypt. The king, as god, had sole rule over the people. He was responsible to maintain justice, peace, and prosperity in the land. By continued refusal to acknowledge the name and power of God, Pharaoh hardened his own heart. The plagues served to demonstrate the impotence of the king both as the ruler and the divine deity to the priests and magicians (10:7), and to the Egyptian populace (12:33). To the Israelites, the plagues were a visual sign of God's power to redeem them out of their bondage and provide for them in the wilderness (14:31).

B. A Look at Leadership

by Edward L. Foggs

Who would dispute that Moses was a gifted leader? The biblical account of his birth, his upbringing, his struggles, his spiritual encounters, his call, and his ultimate assignment all attest to his leadership destiny. "Destined to be a leader" might well be an appropriate epitaph for Moses. His whole life evidences preparation for unique and powerful leadership in the history of Israel and, by extension, in the history of succeeding generations and nations.

Stephen's pre-death witness to his faith in Jesus Christ in Acts 7 includes a stirring and vivid portrayal of the patriarch Moses. Because Moses was such a central, towering, and respected figure in the life of the Hebrews, Stephen spoke at length about the Moses connection in messianic prophecy. The chronology of this discourse gives special insight into Moses' stature as a natural and spiritual leader.

One may appropriately ask several question about Moses. Why had he been born a favored child? Why had his life been spared in infancy? Why had he been reared in the king's palace? Why was he privileged to learn the Egyptian way of life at its highest levels? Why had it been necessary for him to flee Egypt and spend forty years in the wilderness?

Were these experiences merely incidental or coincidental? Or could it be that from birth God was preparing Moses for a mighty mission of leadership? There is ample support for the latter view. Moses' life experiences—from the circumstances of his birth to his "burning bush" encounter—were all a part of his preparation to be God's chosen leader at God's appointed time in God's appointed place.

Although Moses undoubtedly had long harbored a strong desire to see his people liberated from bondage of Pharaoh, quite some time passed before he understood clearly that he was to be the chosen one to lead them to freedom. His burning bush encounter must have brought him great exhilaration of spirit when the Lord said to him, "I have indeed seen the oppression of my people in Egypt. I have heard their groaning and have come down to set them free." His exhilaration, however, quickly turned to apprehension and fear when the Lord continued saying, "Now come, I will send you back to Egypt" (Acts 7:34 and Exodus 3:7-10). Here the call was explicit. "You are to be my leader for this assignment." Moses now is under divine orders, charged with leadership responsibilities he had not sought but for which he had been uniquely prepared.

Whether we call them insights, understanding, lessons, or principles, there is much we can learn about leadership from the life of Moses that is as relevant now as it was at the time of Moses' personal exercise of leadership. For leaders in a scientific, high-tech, know-how society, it is especially important to observe the benchmark of Moses' authority. He demonstrates that however gifted and capable a leader may be, the assurance of God's call is the crowning jewel for effectiveness. Undoubtedly at times the only thing that kept Moses going was the certainty of his call to this particular ministry assignment. Knowing he had been called of God carried its own authority.

Moses' Functions in Leadership

Moses initially objected to God's call, offering excuses of his inadequacy and fears that he might fail in the assigned task. It is not difficult to identify with Moses and his reticence to take on so formidable a foe as Pharaoh. Once Moses could bring himself to accept God's call, however, he pursued the task relentlessly.

29

Character has been defined as the ability to follow through on a commitment long after the mood in which it was made has passed. Moses had character! Long after the excitement of the burning bush and long before the pillar of cloud appeared by day and the pillar of fire by night—in the long "in-between"—Moses met the challenge of leading a people often lacking in understanding and unappreciative of his leadership. On the one hand, he continually had to lift up before the children of Israel the vision of their intended destiny. Meanwhile, he had to coax them on a day-to-day basis with encouragement, reassurance, and discipline.

There is a sense in which the task represents the vision. The leader must always have the ability to see and articulate the faith vision in a manner that inspires others to embrace it as their own and diligently pursue its ultimate fulfillment. However glorious the vision appears, there will be difficulties, obstacles, and hindrances to its realization. Moses knew that liberation from Egypt was not an overnight task nor one he alone could accomplish. Moses, therefore, was a vision-giver, the one who motivated, an inspirer, an encourager, a mobilizer, an administrator, a delegator, and more—all in the name of leadership.

Much of what Moses did, however, Moses learned as he pursued the task and its accompanying maintenance functions. No leader knows it all from day one. As Moses learned from others, we are privileged to learn his lessons less painfully if we are discerning.

Moses' Style of Leadership

How does one "style" Moses' leadership? Key descriptive words evident in his style are integrity, vision, and faith. With these elements, it may be less important whether his style was autocratic, democratic, or reflective of other designating terms. Clearly his style offers much worthy of emulation for leaders of all generations.

In the early stages of his leadership, Moses was counseled by his father-in-law, Jethro, that he was carrying heavier burdens than his leadership required. The counsel of Jethro proved to be lifesaving for Moses (Exodus 18:17-23). Having listened to his father-in-law, Moses soon learned how to surround himself with other gifted leaders. He allowed them the freedom to exercise their ministries even as he exercised his own. Somewhere along the way, Moses made the transition from feeling threatened and intimidated by other competent leaders to feeling secure enough in his call to support other leaders as they responded to their call. This is a critical lesson to be learned and one that could spare the church, in particular, much unhealthy conflict and heartache.

Moses' Leadership Characteristics

The deliverance of the children of Israel from Egypt was not easy. The subsequent journey from Egypt to Canaan was fraught with frustrations, rebellion, ingratitude, and even contempt. Modern leaders need to understand, as did Moses, that the journey from bondage to freedom is never easy. The leader whose task it is to shepherd the transition must be endowed with an ample measure of patience.

Enter Moses—leader of a grumbling, complaining, and ungrateful people who lacked appreciation for their destiny. They even begged to go back to the bondage of Egypt where they would have to bear responsibility for their situation. They could simply blame Pharaoh.

A leader of lesser patience with the considerable gifts of a Moses would long ago have abandoned this crowd. But Moses had committed himself to the task (embodied in the vision) and was further committed to Israel for the long haul. While it is possible to overstay one's time in a given leadership capacity, many leaders push the panic button in the face of adversity and exit long before their vision begins to take shape. Moses understood that perseverance and patience are essential to the fulfillment of faith visions.

Moses' leadership was further characterized by an ability to manage conflict. His dealing with conflict was deeply rooted in an understanding of God's law and God's will for those in dispute. Moses repeatedly brought to his followers a theological context versus a merely political context for dealing with their conflicts.

Throughout the book of Exodus, Moses brings to bear upon the squabblings and conflicts of Israel their covenant relationship as set forth in the Ten Commandments. He challenges them at the points of integrity, social responsibility, matters of justice and mercy, and all of the ethical requirements set forth in the commandments. My conviction is that contemporary resolution of conflict in the life of the church would be much enhanced if leaders were more courageous in establishing biblical criteria for addressing conflict.

Insights from Moses for Modern-day Leaders

All leadership is in some measure situational—situational in that who we lead, where we lead, and how we lead are strongly influenced by situations where we serve. These include situations of time, geography, history, tradition, and perspective. It would be fascinating to contemplate how Moses' leadership might have been different had he lived in another era or under very different circumstances. His gifts were such, however, that he undoubtedly would have emerged as a significant leader regardless of the situation.

Moses models for us a leader in adverse and often discouraging circumstances. He discovered resources beyond himself—both divine and human—to undergird his leadership task. Neither faintheartedness nor self-pity were the trademarks of his style. While he undoubtedly had self interest, he was motivated by a higher calling from which he dared not to veer.

Moses models for us leadership with integrity. There is an evident caring for the well-being of those he leads as opposed to efforts at self-aggrandizement and personal profit. He took risks with the children of Israel that only a person of integrity would feel obliged to take, knowing that embarrassment or even failure could be the result of such risks. (See Hebrews 11:24-27, NIV.)

Moses models for us the skill and spirit of passing the torch of leadership when one's work is done. The temptation for unusually successful leaders often is to hold on and hold on—often until we virtually destroy that which we have given such energy and effort to build. Moses could not cross the Jordan, but he was wise enough to prepare a Joshua to carry on the work to which he had devoted the whole of his life. There is no evidence that Moses passed the torch with bitterness, scorn, ill will, or despair. He stands tall not only because he served well, but because he helped pave the way for that to which he had given himself to outlive him. That lesson alone would spare the church and its leaders the sourness that too frequently accompanies the end of an otherwise illustrious journey.

The unfolding of the life of Moses, especially the events leading up to his call, may well prompt every leader and potential leader to ponder the question, "For what is God preparing me?" The unseemly, the unpleasant, the puzzling and perplexing experiences may well be a prelude of preparation for noble service in the kingdom. The man and the model are worthy of far greater probing than these brief pages present.

Chapter 3
Deborah: Prophet and Judge

A. Deborah

by Marie Strong

Two chapters in the Book of Judges are devoted to the life of Deborah: a narrative account in Judges 4 and a poetic version in chapter 5. The name of Deborah produces visions of strength, indomitable courage, commitment to her religion and her people, and of faith, overwhelming faith. Surely, like Esther she came "for such a time as this" (Esther 4:14).

Time of the Judges

And what was that time? It was a time of low morale on the part of Israel and challenge on the part of her enemies. It was a time before any king or centralized government in Israel. Political control was in the hands of a group of widely separated tribes.

It was a time when Israelite faith was weak and the religions of the enemies were gaining the ascendancy. It was a time when the usual third-generation problem struck Israelite religious life. That problem is well described by the author of Judges: The people served the Lord throughout the lifetime of Joshua and of the elders who outlived him. "After that whole generation had been gathered to their fathers, another generation grew up who knew neither the Lord nor what he had done for

Israel. Then the Israelites did evil in the eyes of the Lord"
(Judges 2:10,11).

It seems to happen rather consistently that the third or
fourth generations fail to have the zeal found in their
grandparents. Apparently, grandpa either had the original ideas that filled him with enthusiasm to act, or the
very struggle produced character. Perhaps the Israelites,
now settled in Canaan, saw no miracles such as those
experienced by Moses and Joshua. Unable to have faith
in the authentic experiences of the past and lacking any
new revelation from God, the people had a "ho-hum"
type of religion.

No great spiritual giants are seen until one comes to
Samuel.[1] He came at the end of the period of the judges.
In writing of that time the author of Samuel says, "In
those days the word of the Lord was rare; there were not
many visions" (1 Samuel 3:1). Visions apparently depend
upon a desire for them, a hungering after God, or as the
psalmist puts it, "As the deer pants for streams of water,
so my soul pants for you, O God" (Psalm 42:1). Or in the
words of Jesus: "Blessed are those who hunger and thirst
for righteousness, for they will be filled" (Matthew 5:6).
Generally speaking in the book of Judges the people
were greatly lacking in the hunger department.

Appearing at least six times in the book of Judges is
the following description: "The people of Israel did what
was evil in the sight of the Lord and served the Baals"
(Judges 2:11). Scholars call this the "formula of Judges."
The outline of the book follows a distinct pattern:

1. The Israelites serve the Baals.
2. They are then conquered by their enemies.
3. They call on their God, Yahweh, for help.
4. God sends them a deliverer, usually called a judge.
5. The deliverer rescues them.
6. The rescue is usually temporary as the people again
worship the Baals.

The whole process is repeated over and over again through the historical period called "The Judges."

Who were the Baals? Baal was the name given to the chief god of the Canaanites. He was believed to be the god of fertility, of rain, of vegetation. There were apparently many Baals. The word means "owner" and each field had its owner or Baal. Nothing would grow without the permission of the Baal of that particular field. It is possible that the Israelites, having been forty years in the desert, knew little about farming. It seems logical to suppose that they asked the people of the land for advice. The people of the land, being Canaanites and Baal worshipers, told them that the land would not produce unless honor was given to the owner or Baal of that land. The problem of the Israelites, first entering Canaan, was possibly more economic than religious.

Since the Israelites at the time were but a loosely organized group of tribes, without any common authority, conquering them was easy. The only unifying factor was their ancestral religion. Unfortunately, at the time of the Judges, faith in their God was weak. There was nothing to hold them together.

Wave after wave of invasion struck the defenseless people. Possibly each invasion affected only a few of the tribes each time. Since there was no central authority to require it, the rest of the tribes did not usually participate in defense.

Each judge was called by God to meet the emergency situation.[2] The qualities for leadership and the impetus for action were given by God. For this reason judges are said to be charismatic leaders. The word *charismatic* has Greek rootage, meaning "grace." Grace is the unmerited favor or gift of God. Each judge was gifted by God for the occasion. Most were gifted for a temporary situation and then seem to fall back into ordinary life. The lives of some of the judges were not exemplary, such as the life of Jephthah, the outlaw and son of a harlot (11:1ff).

37

Deborah Comes on the Scene

At the time of Deborah the invaders were the Canaanites.[3] The Canaanites were a formidable foe. They lived in walled cities, each with an independent king. Surrounded by double walls ten to fifteen feet thick, the cities were impregnable. With few or no weapons the Israelites seemed helpless before their more powerful enemy.

At the time of Deborah, the major Canaanite general was an aggressive leader named Sisera. He had "nine hundred iron chariots" (Judges 4:13). It was to be many years before Israel had access to the iron market. Israelite enemies were so afraid that the Israelites would make weapons that the Israelite farmers were not allowed blacksmiths for sharpening farming tools. The Israelite farmer had to go to the smith of the enemy to sharpen even a plow (1 Samuel 13:19). At the time of Deborah there were no weapons of war (Judges 5:8).

From the phrases "the roads were abandoned; travelers took to winding paths" and "village life in Israel ceased" (5:6-7), one gets the impression of constant raids of main roads, of terrorists attacks on the Israelite population. It was like a modern Lebanon reenacted daily. The result was fear, overpowering fear, and sorrow at the loss of loved ones.

This was the psychological climate when Deborah was called to action by God. In a masculine-dominated culture it seems strange for a woman to lead in battle. It must have seemed stranger still to the editor of the book of Judges for in the Hebrew text three feminine terms are used to describe Deborah. She was Lappidoth's wife, she was a prophetess, and she was a woman (4:4). Although the Hebrew people did not and do not accept women's leadership in religion, Deborah had for years been a judge, in a rather modern sense of settling disputes. "She used to sit under the palm of Deborah . . . and the people of Israel came up to her for judgment" (4:5).

To understand the action of Deborah one needs to comprehend the basic sin of Israel. Israel's major sin was the breaking of the contract she had made with God. There had been an ancient agreement between God and the Israelites. Coming from Egypt to Mt. Sinai, and after being saved by the mighty acts of God, the Israelite people made a covenant with God. The author of the book of Exodus notes God saying: "Behold I make a covenant. Before all your people I will do marvels . . . I will drive out before you the Amorites, the Canaanites, the Hittites, the Perizzites, the Hivites and the Jebusites" (Exodus 34:10-11). The ancestors of Deborah's generation had been saved from Egyptian bondage by God. At Mt. Sinai, soon after leaving Egypt, God told Moses to tell the Israelites, "If you obey me fully, and keep my covenant, then out of all nations you will be my treasured possession . . . a kingdom of priests and a holy nation" (19:5-6). Moses, calling all the people together, gave them these great promises of God. "The people all responded together, we will do everything the Lord has said" (19:8).

Deborah either knew about this ancient covenant or it was revealed to her, for she seems absolutely confident when she says to Barak: "The God of Israel . . . commands you, 'Go gather your men . . . taking ten thousand . . . I will draw out Sisera . . . and I will give him into your hand' " (Judges 4:6-7).

It shows the respect and honor in which Deborah was held, and of course the cowardice and lack of faith of Barak, when he says, "If you go with me, I will go; but if you don't go with me, I won't go" (4:8). Was this the best Israel had to offer; the example of Israelite manhood? Poor Deborah! She did go with him, apparently holding up his weak faith and self-image by her presence, and God did take care of his people just as he promised Deborah. A flash flood on the Kishon River made that small stream a raging torrent. It is described in that ancient poem called the "The Song of Deborah": "from the heavens the stars fought, from their courses they fought against Sisera. The river Kishon swept them away" (5:20-21). What had appeared like strength, the nine hundred chariots of iron, became a severe hindrance. Sisera escaped on foot. He found his way to a tent, the living quarters of a Kenite family [4] (4:17). These particular Kenites had made a peace treaty with the Canaanites. Sisera felt safe. The woman Jael was alone in the tent. Sisera, asking for water, was given milk and went to sleep. Was there an ancient drug unknown to us that produced the deep sleep, thus permitting Jael to drive a tent pin through his head? This fulfilled the prophecy of Deborah, who had told Barak that the Lord would give Sisera into the hand of a woman (4:7).

Deborah's Strong Faith

Deborah was a great leader because she depended upon God in spite of circumstances. Deborah was simply keeping the Israelite side of the Covenant. She obeyed God and God kept his word. He protected them from the enemy. At this time in history the Israelites generally failed to live up to the Covenant agreement. They served the gods of the Canaanites and very soon adopted their weapons in war. Apparently God meant them to trust him for defense. The flood of the Kishon that defeated the Canaanites was an example of the action of God that resulted from the faith of Deborah. The later experience of Gideon, whose only weapons were trumpets and lanterns, was another example of such faith. (See Judges 7:20). It seems clear now that without the strong faith of Deborah, the Canaanites would have taken all of northern Israel and the Midianites would have taken the central area had it not been for the faith of Gideon.

We Christians have a much greater advantage. We have direct access to God. We know from Jesus that God cares. We know that God is Spirit and that we can relate to God because we each have an undying spirit within us. We know that God is all-powerful as well as caring. We have a New Testament that tells us that our response to God should be complete surrender of self, that only through such surrender can true success and fulfillment come. Without such surrender of self there is rather constant irritation and frustration of hopes.

God is all wise. Therefore, one should ask God for wisdom and trust God to take care of problems, great and small. This is true wisdom (see 1 Corinthians 1). To act as though God does not exist, that is, to do one's own thing without God's direction is to be a fool. One is to love God completely and to love the neighbor as one's self. Everyone of every race and kind is a neighbor. These are eternal truths found in the Bible and especially in the teaching of Jesus.

Deborah was able to lead the Israelites to victory because she trusted God and God's wisdom. God honored that trust, and God's power won the battle.

Deborah was also able to trust leadership to another. Surely Barak doesn't appear as a very good candidate for leadership in the kind of program Deborah had in mind. Yet Deborah gave him authority and trusted him with it. It is difficult to train leaders unless they are allowed to lead. Even weak people sometimes rise to great heights when trusted with a task.

Before Deborah appeared, the Israelites were slinking in fear, afraid to go anywhere because roads weren't safe. Many people today are behind barred doors with human-made weapons, fearing to go into streets that are unsafe. Where are the leaders who will trust God for wisdom to solve the problems of today? Jesus said that God clothed the lilies and sees each sparrow fall; will God not also take care of us? (Matt. 6:25-34). Surely it was not nearly as easy for Deborah as for us. She had not heard of Jesus who died for sins. Her route to God was through animal sacrifices. She had no Holy Spirit to guide her. She believed in God and thought all things were possible with God, and her faith paid off.

41

Deborah obeyed God in spite of being a woman in what was definitely a man's world. True prophets and true Christians must give God's message in spite of circumstances and obey even when the cause is unpopular.

When God calls, one should answer. If God calls to the seemingly impossible, one should seek God's wisdom, depend completely upon divine guidance, and follow. God is calling women today just as God called Deborah. God needs women who are fearless and full of faith. Many causes need attention: the drug scene, desperate illnesses such as AIDS, environmental problems, hunger, poverty, and world peace. All of these need the wisdom of God, the compassion of Jesus. God needs leaders who know that anything is possible with God and are eager to carry out God's program. Perhaps we, like Esther and Deborah, have come for such a time as this.

Notes

1. Samuel is not classified as a judge. He came at the end of that period and is better known in his introducing the monarchy.
2. The judges were Othniel, Ethud, Shamgar, Deborah, Gideon, Abimelech, two minor judges, Jephthah, three more minor judges, and Samson. All were called judges, with the possible exception of Abimelech, one of the sons of Gideon who fancied himself a king. (See Judges 9.)
3. The Canaanites are synonymous with the Phoenicians. Before the twelfth century BC they were known as Canaanites, but afterward as Phoenicians. See Ernest Wright, The Bible and the Ancient Near East, Garden City, N.Y. Anchor Books, Doubleday & Co., 438.
4. The Kenites were usually friendly with the Hebrews. They were almost relatives. Jethro, the father-in-law of Moses, was a Kenite.

B. Prophet and Judge

by Deanna G. Patrick

Authority

Following the death of Joshua, the Israelites embarked on a religious roller coaster. They would be unfaithful to God. Then when they faced capture and defeat by their enemies, they would repent of their waywardness and call to God for forgiveness. God would raise up a deliverer who would lead their army to victory over their enemies. During the ensuing peace, they would return to the worship of God. But within a generation they would succumb to the influence of the Canaanite tribes around them and resort to their old ways. This cycle of apostasy, judgment, repentance, and restoration was repeated again and again. During one of the periods of repentance and supplication, God called a woman to deliver the people.

In our first introduction to Deborah, we are told simply that she was a prophet and that she was leading Israel. We must assume that God called her to this special position. Similar judges of the time were described as being "raised up" or "given" by God.

Judges were actually local leaders or rulers and exercised all the functions of a governor. They had both executive and legislative authority. They were also responsible for military action in defense of the clan or tribe. The other judges of the period were primarily military leaders. Deborah was the only one who settled disputes among the people.

Deborah obviously had the skills needed for the assignment. The people respected and listened to her. Their allegiance was voluntary; the authority rested in the person rather than the office. Her charisma drew the people to her. She was their counselor and arbitrator.

The fact that Deborah was recognized as a prophet would also indicate that she was called of God. Prophets were God's communicators, spokespersons chosen to present God's messages to an erring people. All true prophets were called by God. The subsequent victory over the Canaanites would establish the validity of her call.

Deborah's leadership was recognized and accepted by her contemporaries. More than that, she had the authority that rests upon those special persons whom God calls and equips.

Characteristics of Leadership

Deborah knew God. This is her most important characteristic. She knew God's mind and desire for the people. In order for one to know God's will so definitely, one must spend time in communication with God—waiting and listening. Revelation does not often come to those who are not open and receptive. We can assume that in spite of her busy schedule as wife and ruler, Deborah set aside the hours necessary for a close, intimate relationship with God. When the time came, she could say with authority, "This is what God says."

Deborah knew herself. She had a strong self-esteem. She surely was not intimidated by the opinions of others. While she had the following and support of the people as a whole, there had to have been criticism of her because she did not accept the traditional role for women. (There are always critics who disapprove of people who step out of the expected roles; human nature has not changed much in thousands of years.) This was an era in which a woman's primary function was to make a home for her husband and give birth to children—preferably sons. Nothing is said about Deborah's children, but she was a wife. She certainly did not stay home all the time; she spent a good deal of time under a palm tree.

Deborah had the ego strength to accept the call and responsibilities of a prophet. In light of the reluctance of other prophets to answer this call, we must infer that it was a difficult role. A prophet's life was not one that anyone would deliberately seek. Prophets were often despised and ridiculed by the people to whom they were sent to help. Although female prophets were not unheard of in the Old Testament, they were not an everyday occurrence. It would not have been easy for a woman, even one specifically called by God, to rise up and take the leadership role that Deborah assumed. She had to be sure of herself and of her calling and of her God.

Deborah knew people. One cannot be a mediator without knowing human nature. She did not isolate herself from people. She held court under a palm tree that was open and available to anyone who needed help or who simply passed by. She listened to problems, gave advice, settled disputes. She was a mother to Israel.

Deborah knew the law. How else could she make judicial decisions? She was called upon daily to interpret the finer points of the law. She surely had an innate sense of what was right and fair and just. People went to her of their own accord to have their disputes settled.

Deborah knew the situation—the oppression of her people. She must have known it firsthand. She was in the mainstream of the events of the day, not tucked away in a corner. She surely saw the Canaanites racing up and down the highways in their iron chariots until it was not safe for travelers on the main roads. She may have heard her people despair because they did not have the knowledge and skill to work in iron. Among forty thousand in Israel there was not a shield or spear. Her sense of justice would have been outraged at the harassment she witnessed over many years.

Deborah knew whom to call for help. She was able to delegate responsibility. She sent directly for Barak. Maybe he was not so confident as one would hope. He did know how to raise an army. Ten thousand from the tribes of Zebulum and Naphtali followed him. He must have had the ability to inspire confidence in others, even when he lacked it himself, and Deborah recognized this quality in him.

Deborah was decisive. She made decisions quickly, but not precipitously. She had spent time in communication with God and knew God's mind. She did not rely upon her own judgment alone. Her own self-confidence and understanding of the people and situation reinforced her ability to act resolutely. The fact that she was in the habit of making decisions daily also prepared her for major times of testing.

Deborah had courage. She had the courage of her own convictions; she dared to challenge the traditional sexual roles. She had the courage that comes from absolute, steadfast faith in God—courage that enabled her to call forth a relatively weak Israelite army to attack an army equipped with the latest in military armaments. She had courage that prompted her to put her own life on the line.

When Barak wavered and refused to go into battle without her, she did not hesitate. If ever she had wanted to exploit her femininity, then would have been the time. Many other leaders pleaded youthfulness, physical weakness, lowliness of station when confronted with similar calls. She could have pointed out that battle was no place for a woman; practically everyone would have agreed with her. But her response was immediate and positive. She went with Barak and became the inspiration for the troops. She represented the presence of God and kept before them the assurance that God was truly with them.

Function as a Leader

As judge, Deborah's leadership function was primarily maintenance. She held court, and people went to her to have their disputes settled. The oppression from the Canaanites had gone on for twenty years. The people must have lived under a terrible strain with tempers stretched to the breaking point. It was not a time for civil strife; Israelites had all they could do to cope with their common enemies. Thus the need for a judge—a mediator to help in solving petty differences. The hours Deborah spent under the palm tree listening to the complaints and squabbles of the people must surely have made for better living conditions for everyone.

But when the time came to rise up against the enemy, Deborah became task-oriented. God let it be known that it was time to retaliate and she showed no hesitation. She recognized what needed to be done and set about to work toward the accomplishment of it.

Deborah's Style of Leadership

Deborah was an autocratic leader. "She sent for Barak . . . and said to him." She apparently was accustomed to giving orders and having them heeded. But her autocracy was not that of a king or secular ruler. She was God's servant. She did not ask of anyone that which she was unwilling to do herself.

She sat under a palm tree and people went to her for decisions. It is impossible to know her approach to this task. The expression "they came to her for judgment" or "to have their disputes decided" indicates she was also autocratic in her dealings with the people. But this may have been necessary for the time. The nation was young, barely in its adolescence. It is obvious from their history of apostasy and restoration that they were basically un-stable, readily yielding to the influence of those around them. They needed the guidance of a strong leader who could interpret the law to them and direct them in the way they should go.

An autocratic style of leadership is not the most desira-ble. An organization or group, however, requires different styles of leadership at different stages of its development. In the beginning, a group may need a person with background and training who can give decisive direction. A competent autocrat can save time and prevent serious mistakes in judgment.

The danger lies in an overuse of this one style of leadership. A group may remain weak and ineffective, unable to function on its own, always looking to someone in power to give direction. Many churches fall apart when a strong gifted pastor leaves. At the least, their program and ministry cease and nothing is initiated until a new leader arrives.

Deborah spoke with God's authority. Her decrees were prefaced with the statement, "The Lord, the God of Israel, commands you." Such authority gets results. Few dare argue with a leader who declares, "This is the will of God." But the temptation to use this authority to get one's own way is another danger inherent in this style of leadership.

Deborah was an autocrat under God. But she was one as a mother is to her children—settling differences, setting an example, teaching God's ways. Indeed, she was the mother of Israel (Judges 5:7).

Chapter 4
Ruth and Naomi:
Friendship Leadership

A. Ruth and Naomi

by Juanita Evans Leonard

Women's labor accounts for nearly two-thirds of the world's total working hours while their wages account for only one tenth of the world's income. Women own only one percent of the land worldwide. Is it any wonder why women turn to the biblical story of Ruth for a symbol of vibrant, vital leadership? Her story and that of her mother-in-law, Naomi, parallel the lives of ninety-five percent of the world's population who live in or on the edge of absolute poverty. For these "strangers in our midst" a small plot of land on which to grow some vegetables to stave off starvation would be a luxury.

Against the odds, Ruth confronts what seem to the reader impossible odds. Her story tells of the cyclical themes: life and death, feast and famine, loneliness and fullness of joy in complementary relationships. We can identify with her journey, for all of us are confronted with the similiar concerns for life.

What is so unusual about this Moabite woman, a foreigner to Israel, that the compilers of the Old Testament included her story when putting the Hebrew scriptures together? Why document the story of a woman in a particular culture? What does Ruth's story have to offer us in the last decade of the twentieth century? What leadership issues does she raise for women and men who are called to lead the people of God?

Scholars tell us that the story of Ruth took place around 1000 BC and was repeated over and over again from one generation to another. It was put in written form sometime after David's monarchy, perhaps around 500 BC. To think that this great-grandmother of King David was one of two women to have a book of the Bible named after her is to sense the dynamism of her person and God's infinite wisdom. Ruth's story, a woman's story, survived more than five-hundred years by word of mouth and was then put in writing by a man, or men, who by divine providence understood the influence of her character upon the story of the Israelite people. For men as well as women, Ruth's story speaks of the human condition.

The story takes place in a society where a woman was thought of only as property of one's husband and not as a person in her own right. She was like chattel, an object not to be equated with the male. She was a nonperson. The reader begins to get a sense of these conditions in the opening chapter of the story. Hear the story. Listen carefully.

Into the Land of Moab

During the time of the Judges there was a great famine. The search for food in the time of Israel's famine took Elimelech, Naomi, his wife, and their two sons, Mahlon and Chilion, into the land of Moab. The responsibility to provide for his family was of such magnitude that Elimelech risked venturing into foreign land. Soon upon arrival, Elimelech died leaving Naomi and her sons alone. The sons went against the customs of their culture and married Moabite women.

Within ten years, both sons died leaving no children to carry on the family line of Elimelech. Naomi was not only widowed but now had the care of her two daughters-in-law, Orpah and Ruth. Confronted with this dilemma, no one to take responsibility for them and having nothing to eat, Naomi decided to return to the land of her relatives and instructed her daughters-in-law: "Go back, each of you, to your mother's home. May the Lord grant that each of you will find rest in the home of another husband." They were young and would marry again, but Naomi was old and had nothing to look forward to of that sort.

This offer of love was accepted by Orpah, but Ruth declared her own intentions. She radically departed from custom to accompany her mother-in-law into a strange and unknown land—Israel. Ruth's decision to go across cultures and change her geographical home was apparently to forfeit her opportunity to marry and bear children. At risk she became the foreigner. It would mean a life of poverty because no male was responsible for her. She was deliberately choosing to be a nonperson for there was *no* husband and *no* male child to give her identity.

What possessed Ruth to make this choice? The choice was made. She told Naomi that she would follow her God and look after her. Naomi's God was now Ruth's. Ruth knew that Naomi's example of love could only come from the one true God who now compelled her to do what she must do. Ruth's decision came at a crucial time in Naomi's grief and despair. Her loss was devastating. She had been forsaken by God in the loss of her husband, sons, and daughters-in-law. Depressed, lonely, on the edge of starvation with only the smallest hope of returning to the land of her people for some grain, Naomi became silent.

The Return

Naomi knew well the custom of the harvesters to leave grain in the fields for the unfortunate, unwanted ones. This alone was Naomi's hope; what an embarrassing situation for a mother-in-law. But Ruth understood the promise of Yahweh. This Moabite woman had discerned

51

through love what must be done. The uncommon devotion Ruth had for the care of her mother-in-law compelled her to go. As she went, Ruth learned what was to be done so that they would not starve. The storyteller does not let us know if the two women discussed strategies of how they were to survive once they reached Naomi's home area. The only information we have is that upon arrival in Bethlehem, the women of the city came out to greet the strangers and upon a closer look recognized Naomi. "Why it is Naomi, the pleasant one." Naomi responded out of her despair, "Do not call me Naomi. Call me Mara, for the Almighty has dealt very bitterly with me." Naomi had gone away full and returned forsaken by God.

It was not long until the community observed a strange and wonderful sight. The foreigner was gathering grain for Naomi. She was taking her place in the widow's field. Ruth was risking being abused and humiliated by the young men. The effect of the unselfish behavior did not go unnoticed. Soon the news spread, and a relative of Naomi's deceased husband recognized the young Moabite gathering grain from his fields. Up to this point in the story, Ruth had not inquired of Naomi where she was to glean. She knew she had to get busy or they would starve.

Ruth Meets Boaz

Hearing of Ruth's encounter with the owner of the field, Naomi revealed the identity of Boaz. He was a relative of her late husband. A slight hope rose within Naomi and she counseled her daughter-in-law as to her next move. Ruth, however, disregarded Naomi's directions and proceeded on her own. She had been advised to go to the thrashing floor and lie down with Boaz when he slept. He would then tell her what she should do. Instead Ruth initiated the next step in the story. "Spread your skirt over your maidservant, for you are next of kin."

52

Boaz considered her words and in the light of day started proceedings that would lead to the legitimizing of his marriage to Ruth. It was this juncture of the story we witness the same blessing being extended to Ruth by Boaz as we saw given earlier to Abraham. He, too, walked by faith as a foreigner in a strange land.

Within a few months of marriage Ruth conceived and bore a son. The child was presented to Naomi who was made full of joy. The women of the city once again extolled the virtues of Obed's mother to Naomi. "Blessed be the Lord who has not left you this day without next of kin; and may his name be renowned in Israel! . . . For your daughter-in-law who loves you, who is more to you than seven sons, has borne him" (Ruth 4:14-15). How revolutionary—radical—for the compiler of the story to have entered this story in the scriptures. He felt, however, that after such a dark period of history, this love story was warranted. A foreigner, a woman caring for another woman—and to think of the role she played in the salvation history of the Hebrew people.

What Is to Be Learned?

What do we learn about leadership from the story? How might Ruth's leadership apply in our day?

The 1980s and 1990s have become known for their explosion of information. This is never so true as when you look at the bookstore shelves and witness the proliferation of educational materials, books, and cassettes, dealing with leadership concerns. Virtually every discipline, be it business, education, or religion, has its best sellers. *In Search of Excellence* by Tom Peters, *Servant Leadership* by Greenleaf, and John White's *Excellence in Leadership: Reaching Goals with Prayer, Courage, and Determination* are only representatives of the information flood. Articles in magazines and journals cause the reader indigestion as the modern person strives to become all he or she can on the ladder of success. The world of modernity, modernity's eventual downfall.

The tale of Ruth and her leadership offers an impelling note for those who seek a different way. This young widow, herself dealing with the loss of her husband, responds to her loss by putting herself in the place of Naomi, who not only has lost a husband, but two sons, and has no hope of bearing a child. With consummate love she abandons the virtue of obedience to instruction that Naomi had given. True, had she obeyed Naomi, she would have cared only for her grief and future. She subordinated herself in the freedom to love another, however. In that action the story teller reveals an inward determination known to those God directs.

Ruth is going somewhere. She is going to feed and care for her mother-in-law. She will not let her die. She will persuade Naomi's people that they are responsible for Naomi's care; but until they decide and work out the propriety of law, she will be responsible. Ruth has a vision for what must be done and has a strategy to accomplish the task. She takes action!

Scripture reveals the acceptance by Boaz of this compassionate, alert woman from Moab. There is for the reader an awareness of Israel's own journey in a strange land. Israel is compelled to embrace, under Yahweh, the foreigners.

Remember Ruth

Ruth's empowerment through love came through the one true God. She abandoned known customs and gods for her people to go and give to one in desperate need, so that life would be full. She had a vision, a strategy, and took action to give life.

Today the church in society is dying because the gods of modernity have been followed. Today Ruth's story, a story of one who does not seek for her own satisfaction but for a better way, flashes like a strobe light in the dark. A woman powerless in a patriarchal society said no to the dominant cultural theme. She saw a need, she made a plan and carried it out.

Empowered by confessing Yahweh as the one upon whom leaders are to depend, she provides an example of a gifted leader. Those who would be leaders must have a vision, a strategy, and take action. For even though the customs of the society will say no, the motive of love will embrace the foreigner. Who is the foreigner in your midst? What vision, strategy, and action has God given to you? Remember Ruth!

B. Friendship Leadership

by Ima Jean Kidd

How are decisions made? How do visions come to fruition? One aspect of leadership is setting goals, making plans, and taking initiative to accomplish these goals. Ruth and Naomi combined their gifts and knowledge in a collaborative style based on their mutual love and their common goal of building a life together in Bethlehem. Both women were people of action who took risks to make their vision become a reality. Perhaps the most important factors in their success, though, were their acceptance and appreciation of each other's gifts and their cooperation with each other to reach their goal. Likewise, appreciation of differing gifts, cooperation with one another, and initiative are aspects of mutuality that can lead to the accomplishment of goals in the church today. Let's return to the story just outlined for us and consider the contribution of each person to friendship leadership.

Reflecting on the People in This Story

NAOMI—Naomi understood what her daughters-in-law would face as aliens in a foreign land, and for that reason did not ask the two remaining members of her family to accompany her home. As a young woman she, too, had traveled from her home in Bethlehem to the land of Moab. There she and her husband had raised their sons and seen them marry Moabite women. Her husband had died and then her sons, too, died. Her life in Moab had been difficult and painful. She longed for home. Her goal was clear, to make the journey back to Bethlehem and to live the rest of her life in her homeland. She was depending for her livelihood and safety on the system of community relationships her God had established for her people. Although widows and orphans were to receive special care in this system, Naomi saw herself as all alone. She did not presume to ask her daughters-in-law to join her, but rather to bid them good-bye.

As Ruth decided to join Naomi, Naomi's goal became their mutual goal and they formed a powerful dyad. To this partnership Naomi brought more than their mutual goal of returning to Bethlehem. She brought age and wisdom about life, knowledge of God and of the traditions and laws of the community of Bethlehem, the courage to take risks, and an ability to plan strategies. Naomi brought one more important gift to the dyad. She gave them a clear expression of the agony and grief that was part of being a widow and the anger and bitterness that marks life for those who are outside of a community. The clarity of her expression of bitterness was part of the fuel, the energy of the effort. Her need for hope was absolutely essential to the powerful outcome of her story.

RUTH—Ruth made a clear choice to go with Naomi. Her example of decision-making is important to Christian leaders. Before she could make a decision she first had to understand her own values and goals. She valued Naomi and loved her deeply. She valued the gifts Naomi had brought her and determined to remain with Naomi, even if it meant leaving her own home. Ruth based her decision on her values, not on her fears or the risks involved. Perhaps she realized that letting her love for Naomi go undeclared and allowing the older woman to depart from her would, ultimately, be more painful than whatever difficulties the new life in Bethlehem would bring.

Ruth brought several gifts to the dyad, also. Ruth was younger and more energetic. She brought the power that comes from a clear choice to love another human being and to make that love the most important element of her life and their life together. She also gave the dyad the courage to take risks and the hope that their future could be better. Ruth gave clear expression to their desire to have a future together, and her desire for a new life served to balance the bitterness that marked Naomi's lack of hope. One writer compared Naomi and Ruth with Moses, but where Moses led the people to an external Promised Land, Naomi and Ruth are prophetic voices calling the people to an internal Promised Land of mutual acceptance, hospitality, and love.*

BOAZ—Although not a part of the dyad that began the story, Boaz is an important character. He joined the case after Ruth and Naomi had formed a cooperative team. He was a gatekeeper of power. While the friendship and love Ruth and Naomi shared represents one kind of power, Boaz exerted another kind of power. He was a righteous man. Boaz valued the laws of God and of community and honored them. He also brought a gift of gentleness and compassion to the story. He wanted Ruth and Naomi to have enough to eat, and he wanted them to have a position of honor in the community. He recognized himself as related to them, even though Ruth was a foreigner whom he had not known before, and it had been many years since Naomi had lived among their people.

Key Turning Points

Perhaps the most well-known turning point in this story is at the beginning when Ruth gave her famous speech declaring her people, her home, and her God to be those of Naomi. Ruth was not the only decision maker at this junction, although hers is the most clearly seen. Naomi decided to accept Ruth's decision. In the forming of a cooperative leadership team, the acceptance of one another's presence and personhood is absolutely essential to the integrity of the collaborative style. Naomi could have allowed Ruth to come without accepting her presence or contributions. Many so-called collaborative efforts are stymied by the refusal of one or more parties to accept the contributions—the ideas, the gifts, the goals—of the others. So at the beginning of their journey, two decisions were made, an offer and an acceptance.

Upon arrival in Bethlehem, Naomi took a strong leadership role. Her knowledge of the customs and traditions was invaluable. She told Ruth where to go to glean. Naomi was wise in choosing Boaz's field. She not only knew Boaz as a relative, but obviously understood him to be an honorable man. Ruth went to the field to do the work. It was not just the physical labor that she contributed. She accepted the wisdom of Naomi with taking issue; she understood that her physical strength made her the one to go to the field. Ruth also carried with her an attitude of openness. She accepted the help that both Naomi and Boaz offered her. Naomi had decided to make their life in Bethlehem as good for them as possible. She began to plan a way that she and Ruth would be cared for, for the rest of their lives. Her decision to live and build a life with Ruth marked a second turning point in the story. She had moved beyond her initial goal of making the trip to Bethlehem so that she could die in her homeland. The power of Ruth's hope and love had changed her own bitterness and grief. Now, she wanted to live! As relationships grow and develop, both goals and attitudes may change.

Boaz was also a decision maker at this juncture. He saw a stranger and a relative returning after a long sojourn and made a decision not only to obey the ancient laws of God that allowed the two widows to glean the dropped grain, but to go one step beyond the law to instruct his workers to be sure enough grain was left. Boaz became a nurturer. He, too, made a decision based on his values. His values dictated that he do more than the minimum required. His decision to look with favor upon the women came, no doubt, not only from this attraction to Ruth but also from his sympathy for her situation in life and his respect of the elder Naomi, who had survived much. Greed, lack of concern for others, or lack of awareness of what was happening in his field could have prevented Boaz from acting as he did. Boaz was neither ashamed of nor overly proud of his nurturing character. His compassion was simply a part of who he was, and he accepted it as a part of himself. Perhaps his culture, like today's, might not always have seen the ability to nurture or care for as a man's task. Boaz was who he was. An important part of a collaborative effort is for people to be who they are and not strive to be someone else or someone else's image of who they should be.

As the story progresses, Ruth, on the advice of Naomi, did a startling thing. She gave herself to Boaz, symbolically, by going to him in the night. He also was faced with choices. His decision was to protect her reputation and work toward a solution that would give her a place of honor in the community. Ruth had to know and trust Naomi to take such a bold action, and likewise Naomi had to know and trust Boaz to suggest it. They had to know and recognize one another before they could trust. The importance of the community is clear. Naomi knew and understood the values of Boaz as a leader of her people; Ruth knew that Naomi loved her and would not ask her to do something that would be ultimately damaging; and Boaz overcame whatever prejudices existed against strangers and saw in Ruth, a foreign woman, the qualities he sought in a wife. Each took risks and in taking them risked others. An element of collaborative decision making is that no one stands apart from the outcome of the process.

The next scene, at the gates of Bethlehem, is where all three lives come together before the powers of their community. Boaz took action to assure that Ruth would be his wife and in doing so completed the vision that had began as Ruth and Naomi's. The gates of Bethlehem were the center of power, and Boaz was the gatekeeper of that power. He had the power to intervene in the social structure and with the community. His was a social power not unlike that of many larger churches and their leaders. Ruth had the power of certainty about whom she loved and the power of hope. Naomi had the power of years of experience and understanding of human nature and the power of her grief and bitterness. The goal of establishing a new life together might not have been accomplished without all of these kinds of power converging. Power is in the traditional places but also in the complementary personalities and styles of the three people.

The last scene brings in Obed, the new life that would carry Naomi and Ruth into many future generations. The power of this new life at last melted Naomi's bitterness. Not only had they gone home, but they had made a major contribution to the lineage of God's covenant people.

The Presence of God

God's presence in the story is found not so much in God's direct intervention but rather in the action of God's people. God is in Naomi's desire for her people, in Ruth's love, and in their willingness to journey. God is in the community established to care for everyone, stranger and citizen alike. God is in Boaz's willingness to go beyond the requirements of the law to extend compassion. The vision continues. Through the people of God in their caring responsibly for other human beings, God continues to bring about *shalom*.

---

*Margory Zoet Bankson, *Seasons of Friendship: Naomi and Ruth as a Pattern* (San Diego: LuraMedia, 1987), xiii.

Chapter 5
Solomon:
Wisdom/Knowledge/Leadership

A. Solomon

by Thomas F. Pickens

The meeting had been hastily called. To delay the important business at hand could mean danger, possibly even death for Solomon and his mother, Bathsheba. Unfortunately, there was no time for the usual preparations for the coronation of a king. Pomp and circumstance would be present only in a small measure.

King David lay on his death bed. It was only a question of time when he would make that journey from which no one ever returns. In some ways he was looking forward to being at rest with his fathers. The burden of territorial expansion, raising and feeding armies, and governing the tribes of Israel had taken their toll on his body and spirit. He was ready to be at peace.

In his weakened condition, he was unaware that Adonijah, his son, had decided to crown himself as king to replace his father. It was generally known that Solomon was preferred as successor to the throne, but Adonijah felt that if he could beat them to the draw, he could become king and put Solomon and his mother to death to silence them. He could thus eliminate the competition, or so he thought. His plans were well-laid. He enlisted the support of General Joab and Abiathar the priest to help him become king. He hired chariots and drivers, and a group of fifty men to march down the street before him announcing, "Long live King Adonijah."

A Warning from Nathan

Nathan, the prophet, had remained loyal to King David and saw the danger in the clandestine affairs that Adonijah had masterminded. "Bathsheba," he said on one of his regular visits to the palace, "do you realize that Adonijah is now king, and that our lord David doesn't know anything about it? If you want to save your own life and that of your son Solomon, we must go immediately to David and get him to proclaim Solomon as king to reign in his place" (1 Kings 1:11).* Together, Nathan and Bathsheba visited David's bedside to inform him of the dastardly events of the past twenty-four hours and to remind him of an earlier promise that Solomon, son of Bathsheba, should reign in his place. David, obviously disturbed by the news he had received, lifted his weakened body up on one elbow. Gathering his remaining strength, he spoke in a loud voice that could be heard by all who were in the room as he addressed Bathsheba.

"As the Lord lives, who has rescued me from every danger," he said, warming up to the announcement he was about to make, "I decree that your son Solomon shall be the next king and shall sit upon my throne, just as I swore to you before by the Lord God of Israel" (1:29-30, Living Bible).

King David then issued what was to be one of the final executive orders of his reign. He gave detailed plans for the coronation of Solomon, including riding on David's own personal mule, the anointing by Nathan the prophet and Zodak the priest, and culminating in a royal procession in which trumpets would blow, and people lining the streets would shout, "Long live King Solomon."

This was the reason for the haste. Solomon had to be firmly established on the throne and be shown to have popular support before Adonijah and his disloyal group made their way into Jerusalem to take possession. Everything was accomplished in short order, just as David had decreed. When the sound of the celebration reached

Adonijah and his guests, they fled in panic, realizing that their plot had failed. He finally threw himself on the mercy of Solomon and pled for clemency.

Solomon on the Throne

Thus Solomon, son of David and Bathsheba, became the third king of Israel. David, who had reigned forty years, was dead. With the mantle now firmly on his shoulders and the crown on his head, Solomon began to think of the duties that had befallen him. He was the head of a powerful nation. The administrative responsibilities alone could well consume his full time. One of the first tasks to be completed, however, was the building of the temple. David had laid the plans and gathered the necessary finances, but God preferred that someone other than David, who was know as a man of war, carry out the actual construction.

As leader, Solomon would need to keep peace among the various tribes. He would need to make alliances with surrounding nations in order not to be overrun and destroyed. He would need the favor of neighboring monarchs in order to get all the materials and skills necessary for the temple. As he listed the things that would be expected of him, he began to feel like a little child who is suddenly called to accept responsibilities for which he has not had training. Anxious thoughts filled his mind as he realized that his own strength and wisdom, while above average for his peers, were insufficient for the throne. Where could he turn? Who would advise him?

As Solomon contemplated what to do, he remembered that at regular intervals and on certain feast days his people followed the habit of making sacrifices to God. Often when they did this, God either spoke to them or came to them in a dream to instruct and inspire. Gibeon was one of the most popular hilltop altars, and so Solomon went there to follow the tradition of his ancestors.

"Give Me Understanding"

When the sacrifice was completed, God appeared to him in a dream asking, "What would you like for me to give you, Solomon? I am pleased that you have sought me in this manner, and I will grant you any wish in return." Solomon considered this promise. Many ideas ran through his mind as he thought of the possibilities of wealth, power, influence, victories in battles, weapons of war, as well as health and long life. Thoughtfully, but with deep sincerity and honesty, he replied.

"O Lord, my God, you were wonderfully kind to my father, David, and now you have made me the king of Israel instead of him. I am as a little child who doesn't know his way around, yet here I am among your chosen people, a nation so great that they are too many to count. . . .

"Give me an understanding mind so that I can govern your people well and know the difference between what is right and what is wrong. For by himself, who can carry such a heavy responsibility?" (3:6-9).

God was pleased with Solomon's request and did not hesitate to tell him so. "Yes, he said, "I will give you what you asked for. I will give you a wiser mind than anyone has ever had or ever will have, and even though you didn't ask for riches and honor, I will give these to you also" (v. 13).

When Solomon awoke, he realized that he had been dreaming, but that it was really God who had been speaking to him. He returned to Jerusalem intent on following God's plan for Israel and leading his people as a wise king and benevolent ruler.

From that time forward, Solomon became famous for the wisdom he possessed. Not long after he returned to Jerusalem, he was asked to settle an argument between two women over which one was the true mother of a baby. Each claimed that the living baby was hers and that the dead baby belonged to the other woman. Solomon first tried to clarify the claims by restating the facts. "Let's get the facts straight," he said. "Both of you claim the living child is your own and that the dead child belongs to the other." "True, true," they both agreed, looking accusingly at each other.

The king motioned to one of his guards. "Bring me a sword. We will divide the living baby in half, and each of you can have an equal portion." "Good, good," shouted one of the women. "You are a wise king. That is a good solution."

"No, no, please don't do it," the other cried. "Give the baby to her, but please don't kill him." Immediately, Solomon could see the truth of the situation. Insight came easily for him now. Traits of human nature, often hidden to the eyes of the uninitiated became to Solomon obvious clues concerning the subtle motivations that drive people to their desired ends.

"Give the baby to the woman who wants him to live, for she is the mother," Solomon announced as he gently placed the infant in her arms.

Signs of Wisdom

News of this incident spread far and wide throughout the kingdom. People talked to one another about the great wisdom God had given to Solomon. It was comforting to know that providence had decreed that the nation of Israel would be ruled by one who was so favored by the Lord.

There is evidence to suggest that the same degree of wisdom manifested in the incident of the baby was present in other areas of Solomon's reign. His skills in administration were evident in the building of the temple. This undertaking was so great that it required vast resources, both from inside Israel and from surrounding nations. Vast amounts of gold and timber were needed.

Alliances were necessary and the recruitment of men and women to do the construction required the coordinative skills of no less than a genius. Truly Solomon was God's choice for this colossal task.

As the completion of the temple approached, Solomon laid plans for a dedication service. He called in advisers and briefed them about what he had in mind. The service should include the placing of the ark of the covenant in the new temple. This sacred portable structure had represented God's presence with the Hebrew people throughout all the years of their wilderness journeyings. It would be there as a constant reminder of past mercies.

Sacrifices were to be made, choirs were to sing, gifts were to be brought in, and a prayer of gratitude would be led by the king himself. Not only did the advisers agree with the plans and show a high level of enthusiasm, but God himself appeared to Solomon saying, "If you do as I tell you to and follow all of my commandments and instructions, I will do what I told your father David I would do. I will live among the people of Israel and never forsake them" (1 Kings 9:4-5).

The events of the day of dedication are recorded in 1 Kings and in 2 Chronicles in terms that make it one of the most outstanding days in all history. The Ark came to rest in its own room, and countless sheep and oxen were sacrificed. Solomon petitioned God for the forgiveness of the sins of the nation and expressed gratitude for God's wonderful dealings with his people throughout history.

The day climaxed with a scene described as the glory of the Lord filling the temple so that the priests were unable to minister to the people. The voice of the Lord spoke in a solemn reassurance that their prayers had been heard and would be answered. There was great satisfaction throughout the land in the knowledge that they were God's people and that God was guiding their destiny.

Organization and Administration

The organizational and administrative skills of Solomon are clearly shown in several passages in 1 Kings. He divided the nation into twelve administrative districts and placed a prefect in charge of each one (4:7-19). The districts deliberately cut across the old tribal lines to create a higher loyalty and unify the nation under the central government in Jerusalem. The prefects were required to see that the decrees of the king were implemented. Each district had to supply one month's needs for supplies for the king's household (4:27), which included labor for his vast building projects and food for his horses.

Whatever Solomon did, he did with an elaborate, almost flamboyant style. Whether he was gathering gold ornaments and artifacts for the temple walls, doors, and ceiling, or constructing a palace for himself and his large household, he settled only for the highest quality without regard for the cost. The list of provisions necessary for the palace, the number of persons enlisted in forced labor, and the expenditures of vast sums of money all provide evidence of his excesses. Many of the passages in 1 Kings 1-11, and 2 Chronicles 1-9, tend to inform the reader of his excesses rather than leave an impression of his wisdom.

Solomon's internal organization of the nation, however, along with his relationships with Israel's neighboring nations gave him a reputation far and wide as a wise and wealthy king. His vast building projects, including many fortifications, required materials and labor from other nations. His shrewd management of the negotiations leading to payment for these services rank him as one of the wise leaders of that era. His ability to inspire loyalty in those persons accountable to him gave many of his plans a more than even chance of success.

Solomon knew his people to be farmers and shepherds who had neither the manual skills nor the artistic background to accomplish the construction of the temple. Skilled workers and artisans had to be brought in from surrounding nations. He utilized an old loyalty that had been established between his father David and Hiram of Tyre to accomplish some of his goals.

Excesses

The best of leaders often (if not always) have flaws in their character that, even if undetected in their lifetime, are picked up by historians and recorded for posterity. In Solomon's case, both his elaborate tastes and his sensuality weakened his character. These imposed an impossible burden on Israel and eventually weakened its defenses and resources. Twenty cities were forfeited to Hiram in payment for some of the services and labor he had provided. Upkeep for Solomon's seven hundred wives and three hundred concubines was a constant drain on his subjects. His almost limitless power created a type of vanity that was difficult to satisfy fully. Marriage to foreign wives, some for political expedience, led to his establishing altars for the worship of foreign gods. His heart was turned away from the true God of Israel.

The ending of the story as recorded in 1 Kings 11:1-6 is a disappointment when compared with the brilliant beginnings of a young king seeking God for an infilling of wisdom. God, perhaps in frustration with his excesses and his backsliding, promised that the kingdom would be taken from him, but for David's sake, it would not happen in his lifetime. After ruling for forty years, Solomon went to rest with his fathers in the city of David, and Rehoboam, his son, ruled in his stead.

*Biblical material in this section is paraphrased by the writer.

B. Wisdom/Knowledge/Leadership

by Paul H. Rider

"Wisdom is supreme; therefore get wisdom. Though it costs you all you have, get understanding." So says King Solomon (Prov. 4:7). Such words, coming from one regarded as the wisest man ever to live, certainly command our attention.

Knowledge Is Power

Continuing effective leadership demands a certain amount of knowledge and wisdom. Knowledge is power. To know something that another needs in order to perform a task or reach a goal, may place you in a position of determining that person's success or failure. If you have enough knowledge about a given area, you begin to be seen as an expert and can be sought out for your knowledge. Knowledge is the possession of information, which may be significant or insignificant, important or of little value. Sufficient knowledge is tremendously helpful. But, someone has observed, "A little knowledge is a dangerous thing." We might also add that knowledge without wisdom is a dangerous thing. "Knowledge puffs up," Paul says (1 Corinthians 8:1). It can be used to bolster one's supposed position of importance. Knowledge can be used to injure and inflict pain.

Wisdom enables one to make the proper use of knowledge. Wisdom is understanding. It is discerning between good and evil. Solomon prayed for "a discerning heart . . . to distinguish between right and wrong" (1 Kings 3:9). God's answer brought Solomon to an unprecedented position to power, authority, and leadership. He came to be seen as the wisest and most knowledgeable person on earth. From all over the world, people came to hear his presentations on every imaginable subject

(4:29-34). He had wide knowledge of plant and animal life. He was a prolific writer of songs, poetry, and proverbs. One can easily imagine great gatherings of people sitting in rapt attention as Solomon read his poetry and spoke of the mysteries of life. It would be fair to say that Solomon easily qualifies as the great guru of ancient Israel.

In view of all this, we are made to see that Solomon's authority as a leader came from at least two sources. First, he was designated as king by his father David and divinely anointed as king by Zadok the priest and Nathan the prophet. That was a position of unquestioned authority. The king, although ultimately answerable to God, could do anything he wanted. Solomon has to be seen as an outright despot in the use of his power on a number of occasions. But, the right of the king to put to death those who opposed or even questioned him was never to be challenged.

Solomon's greatest authority, however, came from his wisdom and knowledge. He won the hearts and minds of people by simply astonishing them with his intelligence and understanding. He certainly was a genius, and his encyclopedic knowledge kept those who were close to him in awe.

This tremendous amount of knowledge could easily have created a good deal of jealousy and envy in those who had to deal regularly with Solomon. The fact that it did not attests to the wisdom and understanding of the king. Even though he was autocratic in the way he planned and organized the building of the temple, the people were eager to embrace his vision of this magnificent structure. His wisdom in dealing with people must have been a tremendous asset in enabling him to complete the project swiftly.

In matters of foreign policy and international relationships, Solomon was again unequaled. Fear of his power may have influenced his neighbors somewhat, but it is obvious that a deep respect for his wisdom and ability was what gained him most from his neighboring nations. They seemed even eager to provide both materials and skilled workers to help Solomon build the temple and his palaces. In addition to being a leader in his own land, he was a leader among leaders.

It is with feelings of genuine sadness that we see Solomon's wisdom fail him in his most personal and intimate relationships. Wise in matter of state, economics, public policy, and foreign affairs, Solomon is given to utter foolishness in his relationship with his many wives. He turns from the God who gave him wisdom to the heathen gods who led to folly.

To Lead, Know Something

It could go without saying that wisdom and knowledge are essential to leadership. To lead assumes that we have some understanding of where we are and where we want to go. Those who lead know something. But the knowledge possessed by a Christian leader is more than the possession of factual information. The biblical understanding of "knowing" involves an intimate relationship. It has to do with experiencing and involvement with an idea, a person, an object. In scripture, the intimate sexual relationship between a man and woman is referred to as "knowing" one another (Gen. 4:1). With that understanding of knowing, consider some of the areas in which the Christian leader should be knowledgeable.

"The fear of the Lord is the beginning of knowledge" (Proverbs 1:7). We are beginning to know God, when we find ourselves moved to reverence and awe at the consideration of his being. An intimate relationship with God is essential for any Christian leader. Knowledge about God simply will not suffice. The Apostle Paul tells the Ephesians, "I keep asking that the God of our Lord Jesus Christ, the glorious Father, may give you the Spirit of wisdom and revelation, so that you may know him better" (Eph. 1:17). A continuing, growing, intimate relationship with God is considered the norm for any leader in the church. In fact, it is out of the intimacy of that relationship that all other qualities and characteristics grow. It is that vital connectedness with God, in Jesus Christ, that provides the life and power for leadership (see John 15).

Know God and Self

To know God, then, makes it possible to truly know oneself. One of the most dangerous assumptions we can make is that we know ourselves better than we actually do. We can be fairly sure that Solomon never suspected that he could ever turn from the God who had given him so much, to heathen gods who could give him nothing. Self-deception is the easiest deception of all. It is here that the greatest wisdom can fail us. Christian leadership demands that we have a growing knowledge and understanding of ourselves.

But, this understanding should include a great deal more than a knowledge of our weaknesses. The Christian leader is one who has been gifted for leadership by the Holy Spirit. An honest and grateful knowledge of our giftedness leads not to boastfulness but to wise humility. The Christian leader is one who deeply acknowledges himself or herself as created in the image of God and called to give expression to that createdness to the glory of God.

If we have a growing knowledge of who we are, we are well on the way to knowing and understanding the persons with whom we minister and work. We are not surprised by the fallenness of others, because we are well aware of the fallenness within ourselves. To recognize our own potential for evil enables us to deal more effectively with it in others.

But, a leader not only needs to know the potential for evil that resides in everyone; he or she needs to know and be able to see the divine image that is present.

Solomon knew that a real mother would quickly give up her child before she would stand and watch it killed. He was counting on the presence of the divine image when he ordered a baby slain in order to discover its true mother. Effective leadership recognizes that people are capable of both good and evil. Wise leaders look for the good in people but are not overly surprised by evil.

Leadership functions not in a vacuum but in the presence of a multiplicity of influence and forces. As Christian leaders we may not be of the world, but we are certainly still in it. It is a world of great suffering and pain as well as a world of powers and principalities.

God calls the Christian leader to an intimate knowledge and involvement with the suffering masses. The hungry, the homeless, the poor, the suffering are not only to be noticed, but they are to be sought out.

The powers that destroy the principalities where evil reigns, are met by knowledgeable leaders with the understanding that Jesus, who said, "Fear not, I have overcome the world," is with them.

God's Agenda

God has an agenda for his creation. Christian leadership requires a deep understanding and knowledge of that agenda. We are to know what God is about in our world and in our lives. Solomon felt himself commissioned by God to build a temple as a dwelling place for the God of Israel. That divine agenda captured his mind, his heart, and all of his creative energy. He knew what God wanted him to do.

Through a continuing intimate relationship with God in Jesus Christ and a growing knowledge of the Scripture, we can find ourselves equally captured by God's agenda of reconciliation for the whole world.

Christian leaders do not have to know everything. Few, if any of us, will ever be a Solomon. But, we do need an intimate knowledge of some things. A growing knowledge and understanding of God, ourselves, others, the world, and God's agenda, would appear to be basic.

But, greater than knowledge is wisdom. A person may know much about many things, and still be an ineffective leader because of a lack of wisdom. Another, with far less knowledge but much wisdom, may lead with great effectiveness.

Solomon says, "A prudent man keeps his knowledge to himself" (Prov. 12:23). That does not mean he never shares it. He shares it wisely. We are not helped by the person who tries to tell us everything he knows. Wisdom dictates that the other does not likely need all that we think we know. In truth, we may not either. On the other side, wisdom leads us to the awareness that we know a great deal more than we think we know. The wise have learned to be attuned to the intuitive self—to listen to the heart and to be attentive to the quiet and gentle voice of God. Wisdom enables us to sense that there is much more understanding than we have come to possess.

In scripture, wisdom is seen as practical understanding. It is being able to do things rightly. It is the ability to plan and make decisions that accomplish the desired end. Solomon's prayer for wisdom was that he might be able to govern rightly. He wanted to have enough sense to be able to make right decisions. Biblical wisdom is "common sense" growing out of revelation and a direct relatedness and obedience to God. Because wisdom is supreme, Solomon challenges us to get it. We are encouraged to pursue, to embrace, to esteem, and to love wisdom. How do we get it?

Its very definition suggests how it is to be attained. Solomon prayed for it, and it was out of God's covenant relationship with Solomon and his father, David, that wisdom came. James advises, "If any of you lacks wisdom, he should ask God, who gives generously to all without finding fault, and it will be given to him" (James 1:5).

The wisdom needed by Christian leaders is always that which grows out of a close relationship with God. All other wisdom is of the world and foolish. It is the knowing that comes from intimate involvement with God in Jesus Christ, with the revelation of God in Holy Scripture, with the illuminating presence of the Holy Spirit, that gives us the wisdom to live and act rightly in this present world.

Chapter 6
Jeremiah: Caring Leadership

A. Jeremiah
by Arlo F. Newell

Leadership is sought by some while others have it thrust upon them. Such an event in Israel's history is revealed in the meaning of the word *Jeremiah*. James Leo Green has said that it may be interpreted to mean "the Lord shoots!" or "the Lord hurls!"[1]

Launched into prominence during the period of Israel's pagan apostasy (2 Kings 21), the name *Jeremiah* properly identifies God's servant leader. Like his contemporaries Zephaniah, Nahum, and Habakkuk, Jeremiah was sensitive to the culture that surrounded him. His reference to the "potter's wheel" (18:1-6) may be personal as well as apocryphal. The Divine Potter was molding him into a model leader. The sensitive spirit of the prophet was shaped by the suffering of the people, and he could not remain silent (20:9).

Parentage

Born approximately 650 BC of priestly parentage in the small village of Anathoth, Jeremiah was just an hour's walk from the ancient city of Jerusalem. Growing up in proximity to the Holy City, this "son of Hilkiah" (Jeremiah 1:1) was exposed to the many travelers and traders who visited the capital. Education came through traditional and relational experiences. In this setting also he may have met Josiah and Zephaniah. Influenced by religious tradition, the suffering of people, reform movements, and political power struggles, this prophetic leader did not seek but rather was hurled into prominence.

Patterns

Leaders of integrity listen to other leaders. Thus, Jeremiah's prophetic role was profoundly influenced by Moses, Amos, Hosea, Isaiah, and Micah. Especially obvious is the influence of Hosea's preaching. Exposed to the teachings of the prophets before him, Jeremiah was able to articulate God's message more effectively and clearly than his predecessors. Gerhardt vonRad evaluated his leadership as being "far greater in its range and depth than that of any of his predecessors."[2]

Responding hesitantly to God's call, Jeremiah began his ministry in the thirteenth year of Josiah's reign. Called from his birth (1:4-5) the young leader protested because of his youthfulness (1:6). But being assured of God's sustaining strength, he is commanded to speak the Word of the Lord to the nations, "to root out, and to pull down, and to destroy, and to throw down, to build, and to plant" (1:10, KJV). Listening to the voice of God, this leader pursued relentlessly the purpose for which he had been called.

Personality

Leaders lead by the openness of their personal lives, a type of honesty that leaves the leader vulnerable to attack. Such vulnerability is contrary to today's concept of leadership. The humanness of Jeremiah would have caused some in this present hour to turn from him, discredit his leadership, and seek for someone more charismatic and less transparent. We look more for the hero type: the strong spiritual leader who never doubts his or her ability, never questions God, never experiences inner conflict, is always positive, and is continuously successful in whatever he or she may do.

While sometimes desired by the crowd, such leadership is contrary to that portrayed in the life of a Moses, Hosea, Jeremiah, or in the suffering servant passages of Isaiah. Matthew 16:14 indicates that some saw in Jesus this same humanness that was revealed in the leadership of Jeremiah. His loyal scribe, Baruch (36:4), gives us more insight into this leader's personality than we have for any of his predecessors. Heart searching could describe Jeremiah's quest as he sought for personal integrity. Highly introspective, he was constantly seeking to know himself inwardly. Unashamedly he placed his case before God, searching, doubting, confessing, and pleading for himself. Like unto Job, he feared not to call God into court to plead his case before the Judge of the Ages.

In so doing he made this divine/human encounter extremely personal. George Adam Smith wrote, "With [Jeremiah] the human unit in religion which had hitherto been mainly the nation was on the way to become the individual. Personal piety in later Israel largely grew out of his spiritual struggles."[3] In his humanness, Jeremiah often suffered intense emotional fatigue and physical anguish, so much so that at times he could not see beyond the mist of his misery. Here in the wilderness of life's desert experience, the personality of a spiritual leader was being shaped for service.

The sorrow of leadership comes not always from personal infirmity but from identifying with the sufferings of those whom we are called to lead . . . The "Confessions of Jeremiah" found in 11:18-23, 12:1-6; 15:10-21; 17:14-18; 18:18-23; and 20:7-18 are like an open window into the progressive development of this dynamic leader. Mowinckel, the noted Old Testament scholar, classifies these "confessions" as authentic Jeremiah material, saying, "No other prophet revealed the inner turmoil of his heart so much as Jeremiah."[4]

From the opening verses of the discourse until the conclusion of the leader's life we are given a picture of the events that when properly viewed, made him a leader. It is the adventure and exploration of witnessing an immature youth develop into a spiritual giant.

Historical Background

Moral standards are lifted up by spiritual leaders. The Ten Commandments were not too effective until Moses began to lift them up.

Beginning his ministry at the close of Manasseh's fifty-five years of wicked rule, Jeremiah was not ignorant concerning the condition of his culture. Pagan practices were prominent. Syncretism had taken place, blending Judah's faith with the pagan worship of Baal and other deities. In the temples fertility cults were tolerated and prostitution practiced (2 Kings 23:4-7; Zeph. 1:4-6). Decadence continues unabated when there is no leader to lift up a moral standard. Half truths mislead the people. Human sacrifices were being offered (Jeremiah 7:31-32), and the masses of Judah could not discern truth from error.

627 BC to 609 BC

Josiah came to the throne following the corrupt reign of Manasseh. As a young, idealistic dreamer and ruler, he immediately set about to bring reform. By his twelfth year, according to 2 Chronicles 34:3-7, changes were taking place throughout the kingdom. Following the example of his ancestor King David, Josiah sought for a better understanding of God. He was rewarded in the eighteenth year of his quest when workers in the temple discovered a copy of the book of the law (2 Kings 22:3-8), giving guidance in helping to bring about the Josianic reform.

Tearing down idols and halting pagan worship, however, does not constitute true spiritual reform. Josiah's desire was for the purification and centralization of worship in Judah. But when people, priests, and professional prophets have embraced the practices of pagan worship, reform requires a strong spiritual leader. One who will root out—pull down, destroy, build, and plant (Jer. 1:10).

For such a time as this, God had raised up Jeremiah, a youthful, energetic, and inexperienced preacher. With only five years' experience and much zeal, Jeremiah gave his support to the Deuteronomic reform that called the people back to the law of God (11:1-8). While not mentioned as a part of the reform movement, scholars believe that the preaching of Jeremiah and his leadership were contributing factors in the changes brought about by the reform.

Spiritual leadership recognizes both strengths and weaknesses in reform movements. So it was not by chance that Jeremiah saw within the Josianic reform more of a resurgence of Judah's nationalism than that of spiritual renewal or commitment or both. Outward religious conformity did not result in regeneration of spirit. The prophet leader observed the deterioration into empty formalism and dry legalism. Cultic unification and political unification were not viewed by Jeremiah as sufficient to change the course of Judah's history.

Knowing when to speak and when to be silent is a basic indicator of leadership ability. Both of these are observed in this historical period of Jeremiah's life. One is the famous "temple sermon" (7:1-26) as he spoke out against Judah for her superficial repentance. In true prophetic leadership style, he called for drastic surgery to preserve the spiritual health of the nation. The second is referred to as the "silent years" in Jeremiah's ministry. Weiser and vonRad concur in the belief that very little material came from the pen of the prophet during this period. Disillusioned by the reform, persecuted by the people, his time was spent in wrestling with God in prayer and in evaluating his own leadership ability.

609 BC to 598 BC

With the death of good king Josiah, Jehoiakim, acceded to the throne. Unlike Josiah, history records that Jehoiakim was "petty, bloody, selfish, unscrupulous, and ungodly . . . whose chief concern was not the will of God or the welfare of the people, but the gratification of his own wishes."[5]

Under such government and indulgent living, it was not long until the pagan practices of the past became popular again. Jeremiah could not remain silent. There is something about a spiritual leader that will not remain silent when sin runs rampant. With renewed vigor the prophet cried, "Will you steal, murder, commit adultery, swear falsely, burn incense to Baal, and go after other gods that you have not known, and then come and stand before me in this house, which is called by my name, and say, 'We are delivered!'" (7:9-10, RSV).

Getting the attention of the king and his people, Jeremiah was at the same time launched into the light of prominence on the stage of life. From that time forward he would become the critic and counselor of royalty (22:1-9, 13-19).

Prominence does not preclude persecution for the spiritual leader. Jeremiah, under the last years of Jehoiakim's rule, was barred from the temple. Burning with desire to speak (25:1-ff), Jeremiah enlists the aid of Baruch as a scribe to recorded his messages and carry them into the temple. Though deprived of speaking, the true leader emerges as he finds a way to communicate his message to the people (597 BC to 587 BC).

The third king under whom Jeremiah served was Zedekiah, a weak, vacillating, easily influenced individual. Needing help and soliciting support, the king was somewhat considerate of the prophet. Jeremiah anticipated improved relationships and conditions within the kingdom. Although willing to consult with Jeremiah and to receive his counsel (37:17-21; 38:7-28), the king was too weak to control and too fearful of public opinion to attempt to make changes for the good of the people.

Grasping for political strength, Zedekiah violated his agreements with Babylonia and made alliances with neighboring countries in hope of breaking free of Babylon. As a courageous leader, Jeremiah counseled Zedekiah to surrender to Babylonia. Rejecting his counsel, the prophet was then seized by Zedekiah's guards, placed in stocks, beaten, thrown into a slimy cistern, and left to die.

Even this punishment did not silence the leader's voice. Rescued from the cistern by the interventions of King Zedekiah, Jeremiah once again proclaimed the same message. His message? Judah should surrender to Babylonia in order to spare Zedekiah's life and save the holy city. When this plea was rejected, Jerusalem was destroyed, Zedekiah was taken captive, his family slain, and the king carried off into bondage and death. Nebuchadnezzar, king of Babylon, left only a remnant behind. Once again, Jeremiah exemplified the quality of a true spiritual leader by remaining with the people in Jerusalem. Working with the newly appointed leader, Gedaliah, the prophet joined in rebuilding the city (40:1-6).

Post 587 BC

Jeremiah could have returned to Babylon with Nebuchadnezzar, living out his life in comparative ease and honor. His decision as a leader, however, was not to secure his own comfort but to exercise his gifts in a manner that would benefit the people of Judah, thus fulfilling God's higher purpose. Servant leadership makes decisions based upon God's will and ministry to people in need. It was during this temporary period of peace under the new governor, Gedaliah, that Jeremiah produced some of his greatest positive works. Referred to by some as messages of "consolation," the emphasis was upon the hope that helped Judah through the critical crisis of reconstruction.

Chapters 30 and 31 particularly demonstrate the positive posture of a leader. Jeremiah assured them of God's continuing, constant care and the reality of rebuilding Jerusalem. "I have loved you with an everlasting love; therefore I have continued my faithfulness to you. Again I will build you, and you shall be built.

"I will turn their mourning into joy, I will comfort them, and give them gladness for sorrow" (31:13).

Leaders also invest in what they lead others to believe. In an attempt to convince people that he believed Jerusalem would rise again, the prophet purchased property, anticipating fulfillment of his prophetic message (chapters 32-33).

But his ownership was short-lived. In an act of sedition, Gedaliah was assassinated and the perpetrators, seeking to escape punishment, fled to Egypt, taking with them as captives Jeremiah and Baruch. Leadership that is authentic is not limited by geographical boundaries, political personalities, or seasons of the year. To Jeremiah, wrong was wrong, whether in Babylon, Jerusalem, or Egypt. Being forced to reside in Egypt did not silence his voice against the idolatrous practices about him. Primarily preaching to the remnant of Judah, his message also reached others as he sought to his final breath to "tear down and to build up," to "pluck out and to plant." Having leadership thrust upon him as a child, Jeremiah confidently walked off the stage of history, leaving the witness of a martyr that mattered, a true leader, giving to us lasting lessons in leadership.

A Legacy of Leadership

The lessons revealed in this prophetic writing are adequate for the twenty-first century. In the recent book, *A Passion for Excellence*, coauthored by Tom Peters and Nancy Austin, reference is made to transition taking place in today's leadership. The authors review the past, focusing on the style of leadership known as MBO, management by objective. Seeking to achieve a particular objective, leaders were sometimes guilty of forgetting the people with whom they served and others who looked to them for leadership. People were sacrificed because the goal or objective consumed the leader.

Surfacing in leadership today, Peters and Austin believe, is what some call MBWA, management by wandering around. Here is a leadership style at least as old as Jeremiah. As a leader called of God, he wandered around with these unstable Israelites, seeking to give direction in the difficult days of Diaspora. But without this insight gained by wandering with them under the varied styles of political and religious influence, he could not have clearly communicated God's message. Servant leaders walk where the people walk, as prophets have always done, and they sit where the people sit.

These lasting lessons from Jeremiah are multiple but simple; they are profound but practical. To lead in today's world, one would do well to emulate this one who was launched into leadership. Here are seven lasting lessons in leadership that surface in the careful study of Jeremiah's ministry.

1. Leaders are humble, recognizing that the source of strength is not in themselves. Such persons practice prayer, tapping into the eternal Source of all power and wisdom. Dependence on God does not allow for self-pride and arrogance to dominate one's life.

2. Leaders are sensitive to the needs of others, entering into their lives with them. Moved by human need, sensitive leaders are not ashamed to cry or to express their emotions. Jeremiah cried, "Oh that my head were waters, and my eyes a fountain of tears, that I might weep day and night for the slain of the daughter of my people!" (9:1, RSV). Spiritual leadership cannot afford the luxury of becoming calloused to the needs within and without the church.

3. Leaders are called, not purchased. Authentic spiritual leadership is evident when the leadership is being exercised without the possibility of personal monetary gain or glory. Jeremiah could have become wealthy in Babylon or Egypt but he willfully, intentionally, and deliberately chose to remain and identify with the people of God, even at great personal sacrifice.

4. Leaders inspire others with positive, affirming messages of hope. God's people are led, not driven with fear or promises of health or wealth. Unashamedly, Jeremiah pointed out the weaknesses of Judah, but he was not trapped by the negatives, subjecting the people to low self-worth. In the most difficult days he lifted up the light of hope.

5. Leaders are consistent, giving security in the midst of the storm. With the transition of power in political rule, Jeremiah could not allow himself to be "tossed to and fro by every contrary wind" or by the trends of the times or the popularity of programs. Neither the man nor the message changed throughout his leadership.

6. Leaders listen to the inner law and to other reliable leaders. Hosea influenced the life of Jeremiah, and the prophet listened to what had been said. He learned from other prophets, but he was not enslaved by the past. Jeremiah also listened to his heart: "I will put my law within them, and I will write it upon their hearts; and I will be their God, and they shall be my people" (31:33, RSV). The person that would lead must be able to hear the beat of another Drummer.

7. Leaders are willing to die for what is right. To believe in what one seeks to achieve becomes the motivation that pulls us onward and upward. The scientist, athlete, scholar, or servant of God who really believes in what

he or she is doing will gladly pay the price. Spiritual leaders, following the lessons of Jeremiah, will not be defeated by poverty, peer pressure, persecution, or other personal peril. His example was that of a true leader, willing to die for the cause. "Tradition tells us that he was stoned to death in Egypt by the Jews who carried him there because he preached against their idolatrous practices. HE WAS FAITHFUL TO HIS CALL TO THE VERY END."[8]

Notes

1. James Leo Green, *Broadman Bible Commentary*, Volume 6, "Jeremiah-Daniel," (Nashville, Tenn.: Broadman Press, 1971), 6.
2. Gerhardt vonRad
3. George Adam Smith, *Jeremiah*, (New York: Harper and Bro. Publishers, 1929), 5.
4. J. A. Thompson, *The Book of Jeremiah*, (Grand Rapids, Mich.: Eerdmans, 1980), 38.
5. James Leo Green, *Broadman Bible Commentary*, Volume 6 (Nashville, Tenn.: Broadman Pr, 1971).
7. Nancy Austin and Tom Peters, *A Passion for Excellence,* (New York: Random House, 1986).
8. C. Paul Gray, *Beacon Bible Commentary*, Volume 4, Isaiah thru Daniel (Kansas City, Mo.: Beacon Hill Pr, 1969).

B. Caring Leadership

by Joseph L. Cookston

Basis for Leadership

Jeremiah describes without equivocation the event that plunged his life into a leadership position from which he would never escape: "The word of the Lord came to me" (Jeremiah 1:4, NIV).

The call to leadership was dramatic. First, Jeremiah argued with God that he didn't know how to speak well, then that he was too young. Jeremiah heard the Lord's rebuke of his doubts and received the life-long promise that the Lord would be with him and rescue him. The calling event climaxed as the Lord reached out and touched Jeremiah's mouth and deposited the words Jeremiah would utter. In those dramatic, intimate moments, Jeremiah received his appointment, the outline of his task, and his commission to be the Lord's mouthpiece to the nations of the world.

The call could not be avoided. Jeremiah experienced the compelling nature of the hand of God upon the life of a servant chosen for a specific task. The call to leadership contained two object lessons, the branch of an almond tree and the boiling pot, with accompanying pronouncements against Israel and Judah. The Lord summoned Jeremiah to stand up, to get ready, to resist being terrified and promised through all that followed he would be with Jeremiah and rescue him. The divine impulse could not be quieted. Later in his prophetic journey, Jeremiah experienced second thoughts about proclaiming the awful words of the Lord and decided to be silent for a period of time. Try as he might he could not. He was controlled by an inescapable compulsion to be the mouthpiece of the Lord. "His word is in my heart like a burning fire, shut up in my bones. I am weary of holding it in; indeed, I cannot" (20:9, NIV).

From his discourses with the Lord and his inner thoughts recorded in his poetic writings, we catch glimpses of a man who was responsive to the wayward-ness of his people. There was something within the brooding, sensitive human side of Jeremiah that would align him naturally with the divine summons. Jeremiah wrote as one who had compassion for the leaderless and unknowing people around him. Though he decried their wanton abandonment of the ways of the Lord, Jeremiah pleaded with his nation to unstop their ears. "O land, land, land, hear the word of the Lord!" (22:29, NIV). Accompanying his divine summons, Jeremiah brought to his call to prophetic leadership a realization of the void of God-centered national leadership and an ambivalent on-again, off-again penchant to fill that leadership gap. Jeremiah's disappointment with the nation's response to his warnings may give indication that he thought he could make a difference. When his warnings went un-heeded, the human side of Jeremiah was ready to capitu-late.

Leadership Style

To a certain extent Jeremiah's circumstances dictated his leadership style. The prophet, particularly the prophet with an unpopular message, did not gather a large follow-ing of people. Though his message generated ultimately from a heart of concern and compassion for the well-being of the people, the content of the message cut deeply across the grain of national pride and religious practices. The pathos within Jeremiah evoked in him an anger, yet an anger that found its release more often than not in sympathy rather than in retaliation.

As we ponder Jeremiah's leadership experience, some interesting questions arise: What is the style of leadership when no one follows? Does leadership imply that some person or group of persons will respond? What do you do when no one follows? Definitive answers to these questions may not be possible. Nevertheless, Jeremiah's account may give us some good clues.

Jeremiah aimed his message at different kinds of audiences. He preached to the masses in public places: on the temple steps, in the temple courts, by the city gates, in the city streets. He called together smaller groups at particular meeting places that helped to demonstrate the content of his message: at the potter's house, in the king's courtyard, in a temple side room with leaders of the Recabites. He spoke privately with civic and religious leaders: to Pashur, the chief officer in the temple; to King Jehoiakim; to a prophet, Hananiah. He wrote letters to those in Babylonian exile.

Although there are indications that Jeremiah may have been a part of a small prophetic community who welcomed and shared his message, the record portrays Jeremiah working primarily alone.

Probably more than any other style, Jeremiah worked from a servant role mind-set; he was a servant bound to the Lord and unheeded by his people. Though vengeance sometimes heated his words, Jeremiah pleaded with the Lord for the sake of the people. Though on occasion his words rang with destruction and wrath, the cause for his pronouncements were not his personal vendetta so much as his deep care for the nation's people. His own tears and suffering welled up from his deep concern for the faithfulness of the nation rather than for his own gain or vindication.

The mark of his leadership could be measured not so much by what was seen but by what was not seen. Jeremiah led the way for the conscience of the nation of Judah to be restored, to regain its foothold on the pathway of obedience to the Lord. His was a voice that would not be silenced by his death. His words would ring in the ears of the Exiled, be quoted more than any other prophet by Christ, and foreshadow the establishing of the new covenant by Christ centuries later. Jeremiah continued to lead though no one followed.

Leadership Function

At first, the thrust of Jeremiah's words and actions was to induce change in the religious and social structures of his day. He was not pleased with the status quo. His was a call to radical change, a returning to obedience to the Lord. His function was to call a complacent nation to wake up and to tune into the movements of God through the changes in history that were imminent and taking place all around them.

Jeremiah rooted his message in the past. The Lord had spoken and made a covenant with Israel. The Lord has been faithful to Israel, has been as one betrothed to her, has delivered her from her enemies. But Israel's ancestors chose to accept the religious pluralism of their surroundings and forsook allegiance to the Lord. They worshiped at the convenient shrine centers that dotted the agrarian countryside.

Jeremiah's message described the present. The pattern of idolatry had not changed. Israel continued to pursue religious, social, and military absorption of pagan cultures. The current state of affairs was abhorrent to the Lord. "Return, faithless Israel . . . acknowledge your guilt . . . you have scattered your favors to foreign gods . . . and have not obeyed me," declares the Lord (3:11, 13, NIV).

Through the years, Jeremiah's message changed as Israel continued to ignore the Lord. Military forces escalated on the borders of Judah and powerful war machines approached the walls of Jerusalem. Jeremiah announced the news that Jerusalem and its inhabitants would be captured and taken to an unknown land; and he consoled the soon-to-be captives with words of hope, words that would give them solidarity during the years of their captivity. Yes, the God of all the nations was changing

93

national governments. Yes, God was bringing about a kind of demolition throughout the known world. But God was destroying in order to build up, to plant again. Yet that same God still had his eye upon Judah and would not forsake his people even in exile. In a countryside besieged by the enemy, Jeremiah illustrated the promise of return and hope by purchasing a plot of land for use by generations to come.

Though his message altered somewhat as the political scenarios advanced, Jeremiah's leadership orientation was anchored in what might be called the future present, where the present meets the future. He focused on the tasks necessary today that will bring to fuller light God's desires for his people. The routine of life can be mesmerizing, and God's people in any age can veer off course seemingly with little effort. The church will be helped as it heeds the voices of contemporary Jeremiahs and looks seriously at the influence that attitudes and practices today will have on the direction that tomorrow will take.

Leadership Characteristics

Reliance Upon God. Jeremiah was sustained by his life with God. Such was the promise of God to Jeremiah at the outset of his ministry, and the prophet left us the record of how it was fulfilled. In it we see that God, by separating Jeremiah from all human solaces and surrounding him with enemies, had thrown him wholly upon himself. The prophet had literally nothing left but God. To God therefore his burdened soul had recourse in constant prayer and meditation. These transactions he pictured as dialogues in which God and he talked freely with one another. Thus he obtained companionship, relief, encouragement, assurance, and all that he needed in order to go on.

One instance reveals the candor with which Jeremiah contends with God about his troubles. The dialogue followed on the heels of stinging accusations by powerful, wealthy leaders of his day. Jeremiah brought into question the justice of God when he asked, "Why does the way of the wicked prosper? Why do all the faithless live at ease?" (Jeremiah 12:1, NIV). He pointed out to God that he had been tested and found to be true, yet he had experienced no prosperity. God's answer brought no comfort: "If you have raced with men on foot and they have worn you out, how can you compete with horses?" (12:5, NIV). It was a stern answer, with no concession in it, not even comfort, but only an iron demand: "Let go of complaining; these enemies are as nothing."

Not all of Jeremiah's devotional life concentrated on contention and complaint. In his solitude with the Lord his soul uttered lofty praise and gratitude for the steadfast love and faithfulness of God. Jeremiah was convinced that ultimately God loved deeply and cared strongly for the world's peoples.

Words such as these cradle the gloom of Jeremiah's message in the assurance of a God who works among all peoples with a divine benevolence. "O Lord, my strength and my fortress, my refuge in time of distress, to you the nations will come. . . . Therefore I will teach them—this time I will teach them my power and might. Then they will know that my name is the LORD" (16:19-21).

International Outlook. Jeremiah came to leadership with an outlook that superseded the preoccupations of his society. He understood the movements of the Lord from a broader perspective that included other nations and their leaders. He was bounded neither by national arrogance nor traditional preservation tactics. He viewed the activity of God as encompassing all of the world's peoples, and though God had selected a people to share his favor, sometimes that favor meant discipline and suffering for a while. The prophet was set "over the nations" and had a commission to participate in that divine plan throughout the known world.

Compassion. Jeremiah had compassion for people.

The sad irony of the case lay in the fact that Jeremiah's disposition seems to have been companionable and friendly. The last thing he wanted was to be solitary, much less hated. His message of doom was none of his own choosing; in fact, he interceded to the Lord on behalf of the people on many occasions. Because the people were crushed, he was crushed. Day and night he cried tears like a fountain for those who would be destroyed. He agonized with his people to listen to the Lord. In the course of the forty years or so of his prophetic leadership, Jeremiah held firmly to the conviction that God was a God who ultimately loved all people and Jeremiah could do none the less.

Suffering. The privilege of God's call to leadership held no honor for Jeremiah. We see no halo of any kind around the prophet's head, no ravens feed the prophet in his hunger, no angel stops the lion's mouth. In his abandonment to his enemies Jeremiah is completely powerless—neither by his words nor his sufferings does he make any impression on them. There is no happy ending.

Near the end of his prophetic life, these words came to Jeremiah's secretary, Baruch: "You said, Woe to me! The Lord has added sorrow to my pain; I am worn out with groaning and find no rest. The Lord said, Say this to him: This is what the Lord says: I will overthrow what I have built and uproot what I have planted, throughout the land. Should you then seek great things for yourself? Seek them not. For I will bring disaster on all people, declares the Lord, but wherever you go I will let you escape with your life" (45:4-5, NIV).

At this time of judgment, when God has to tear down his own work in history, no human being can look for any good for himself; it is no wonder that the prophet was drawn in a quite exceptional way into this demolition. Here a human being, Jeremiah, has in a unique fashion been called to bear a part in the divine suffering.

This aspect of Jeremiah's leadership call is perhaps the most difficult for moderns to comprehend. The image of the suffering clashes with the popular image of a leader. The suffering leader does not sparkle well in the acclaim of the limelight accolades and does not find miraculous answers to problem situations. The suffering leader must deal with the ambivalence of caring for people and yet delivering what may be an unpopular message. The suffering leader must know the pain of wounds and unresolved tensions. The suffering leader will out of necessity come to know complete reliance upon the Lord.

Certainly the church can be strengthened in these times by persons who understand the call to leadership from a position, like that of Jeremiah, of weakness. These are they who know the paradox of healing through suffering and who discern the breadth of God's activity that is greater than any particular religious tradition, local congregation, or denomination.

Conclusion

More than all the "words of the Lord" to Israel, Jeremiah left to posterity his life with God. And what a life with God it was! Even today, with all the succeeding ages of Jewish and Christian devotion for us to draw on, it holds us by its sincerity, its intensity, its surrender, its vigor, its freedom, its intimacy. But the most appealing quality about it is its humanness. The very weaknesses of the man, so simply revealed—his petulance, his timidity, his perplexities, his cries of pain, his calls for vengeance, his desires to give up—bring him close to the common heart. And the way in which he overcame them is what everyone knows deep within to be the true way. Again and again we can turn to Jeremiah's dialogues with God when our own strength runs low.

Chapter 7
Elijah: The Prophet Leader

A. Elijah

by Gertrude Little

You may search diligently through the table of contents of your Bible yet find no book written by or carrying the name of the highly revered prophet Elijah. Nevertheless, he is considered by most biblical scholars as a pivotal figure in preserving for the world the monotheistic religion and the ethnic group known as Israelites then living at the eastern boundaries of the Mediterranean Sea.

This perceptive, sensitively spiritual prophet heard the voice of the Almighty Creator as he tramped the high places of the wilderness of Tishbe east of the Jordan. Then he would descend like a whirlwind to convey what he believed to be God's message for his people. He knew himself to be God's spokesperson—a prophet.

Trouble with a King

This mountain herder declared on one eventful occasion, "As the Lord Almighty lives, whom I serve, I will surely present myself to the king today." The king of Israel was Ahab. The year was somewhere between 869 and 850 BC. The issue between Elijah and Ahab was religious syncretism, considered apostasy or idolatry by Elijah, which the king and his wife were seeking to inaugurate as official in the whole of Israel. They wanted to merge the worship of Yahweh and Baal to bring unity in their land.

This wife Jezebel, a sophisticated Phoenician, had nothing but contempt for the simple, austere worship of Yahweh that the Israelites had learned about from their ancestors Abraham, Isaac, Jacob, and Moses. It had no images or other human-made ceremonial objects or persons.

After Jezebel had been married to Ahab and converted him to her views, they set about to convert the court of the king to the cult of her god Baal. Ahab did little to assist her but nothing to prevent her evangelistic activities. She ordered temples built to Baal and prophets, priests, and prostitutes brought from Phoenicia to set in motion the new religion.

The philosophy promulgated to the people was that they could worship both Yahweh and Baal. This was the compromising syncretism Elijah saw as undermining the true religion of the Israelites. So he went among the Israelite people preaching, crying out for them to repent and turn again to the faith of their mothers and fathers.

Many of the people in the Israelites' territory were descendants of Canaanites. Generally speaking they considered it proper to worship either Yahweh or Baal or both simultaneously. Many church people in our time think similarly except instead of Baal they go searching for life's ultimate answers in yoga, astrology, eastern religions, and a whole register of so-called New Life cults, all the while professing their Christian faith. Syncretism is a continuing problem when religious people get their attention drawn away from the creator God and his Son the Lord Jesus Christ.

All of this confusion in Israel stirred Elijah's religious ire. It led him to exercise all his God-called prophetic energies to warn the remnant of his people, yet in the land, of their need to turn again wholeheartedly to Yahweh.

The Elijah Stories

The biblical books, 1 and 2 Kings, included several stories of Elijah's activities. Such stories may have been handed down by word of mouth but not recorded by Elijah himself. In them we search for the real and revered Elijah.

A series of brief narratives is known by Bible students as the Elijah Stories. We may need to ponder long on some of them to find God's messages for us regarding leadership. Elijah's experiences are hardly models for us in our own historical setting.

At the time Elijah made his first public appearances a devastating drought was ravaging the area where he traveled. One of Elijah's first encounters with Ahab was to tell him, "There shall be neither dew nor rain these years, except by my word" (1 Kings 17:1, RSV), and indeed there was none for three and a half years. Ahab would know Elijah spoke as God's spokesperson, his prophet.

The *El* in Elijah's name is the general name for the "high God." To both Elijah and Ahab the high God would be Yahweh. The message of the salvation of the high God had been brought by his messenger Elijah.

The high God, Yahweh, was the first God in the perception of the Israelites. Their neighbors had many baals—offspring or appointed spirits of the overarching Baal whom Jezebel was now trying to bring them to worship.

Elijah carried the then-known world's greatest message, which was that the Israelites would be saved for Yahweh's kingdom if they would desert all these pagan gods they had been exploring and repent and return to the worship of the high God, their creator and benefactor.

In the Face of Drought

No drought would stop Elijah. He would be obedient as always. He would even accept food provided for him through the hated, gluttonous ravens who may have been the only surviving animals in the stricken area. Nothing obliterated his sense of obligation to carry this divine call.

Elijah was resourceful. Many would have given up hope and died in the face of a drought that lasted years in a place where he was accustomed to finding rushing torrents on their way to the Jordan River. It is even possible the ravens at first may have viewed him as prey, but he and the Lord turned that eventuality about.

We are faced yet again with the understanding of the miraculous by Elijah. We watch him as he experienced God's using the unlikely to benefit his children. Like Elijah we are offered an opportunity both to receive and to give at God's hand.

In his solitary trust with God, Elijah was on an inward journey of preparation to act and hear from God, first for himself and then for at least two others named in the biblical account. Two more persons were added to his circle when he allowed God's power to work through him for the benefit of a widow and her son. Later he would be called upon to be the channel through whom God's power could be demonstrated and experienced by a larger number of people.

Elijah's leadership training was progressing. In this drought time period (ninth century BC) Elijah learned to be flexible. When the water in the brook Cherith dried up and the ravens sought water for their thirst elsewhere, his source of food and drink also disappeared.

On to Sidon

We cannot be certain he then expected another miraculous provision for his need. But we do see that he does not depend on himself alone. He believed God directed him to go and live in Sidon at a city called Zarephath.

Sidon was at the northernmost point of Phoenicia with a seaport and was hence a trading center. The land area was often called Sidon instead of Phoenicia. Probably most significant to Elijah was that the father of his chief Phoenician enemy, Jezebel, was king of Sidon when Jezebel was given in marriage to the Israelite king, Ahab. Imagine Elijah's feelings when he was called to go deep into enemy territory to the chief city of Jezebel's youth and training to overcome his own people, Israel—to capture them for the god, Baal, or his female counterpart, Ashtarte. Both of these pagan deities were heads of groups of gods worshiped in different countries. Each of these lesser deities usually carried in their names the name of Baal or Ashtarte. The deities worshiped in Canaan were usually fertility gods related to plants or animals native to the land.

Elijah would perceive why God directed him to go to Sidon. The Phoenicians had been developing this area immediately along the Mediterranean coast in Palestine since 1200 BC. It was now at the height of the culture of that time. The city to which Elijah was to go was Zarephath. It was eight miles south of Sidon and twenty miles south of Beirut.

The area was well irrigated by a system using both the rushing streams of the nearby mountains and underground streams. Little land was suitable for tillage. What was there produced wheat, grapes, olives, figs, and similar fruits requiring little land to support the trees and vines. But these grew in profusion from year to year. Flocks of sheep and goats grazed on the hillside. At some time Elijah would have hiked on these hillsides and would know he would find food here. He would also know he would have hearers and followers among the sheepherders, being one himself. He wanted them to hear God's message and decide to worship God even though their native religion may have been Baalism.

Another purpose he would have would be to reach any Israelites who may have come to Sidon to secure a livelihood. His passion was to lead all Israelites away from the same pagan worship Jezebel and Ahab had been promoting in Israel. He was becoming ever bolder as a prophet of Yahweh. He was preaching repentance—turning again to God's command to worship God alone.

As Elijah approached the gates of Zarephath he saw a woman gathering firewood. He suspected she might have food since she lived in this rich province. So he called to her to bring him a drink. Then when she responded positively, he asked her for bread.

But the widow's desperate reply was, "I have nothing baked, only a handful of meal in a jar, and a little oil in a cruse; and now I am gathering a couple of sticks, that I may go in and prepare it for myself and my son, that we may eat it, and die" (17:12).

Elijah, as a spokesperson for God, saw an opportunity for her to cooperate with God and the prophet. He instructed her to make a cake for God's messenger and then for her family. He assured her God would supply meal (flour) for their sustenance until the rains came again. She agreed and they had sufficient food.

But the son of the family became ill. According to the way primitive and sometimes modern people often think at first, this performer of God's miracles must see some evil in her life and be punishing her by sending illness to her son.

Elijah carried the sick boy up to his own room in the loft and prayed earnestly that God would heal him. At the same time he used what we would call artificial respiration, for the boy had ceased to breathe. When Elijah had done these things, the boy was revived and restored to his mother. Then the mother was convinced Elijah was truly God's spokesperson. Elijah had given as he had received of God's grace and spirit. He had reached out beyond himself to be an instrument for good in God's hand.

As the drought that had besieged Israel for more than three years approached its end, the Lord instructed Elijah that the time had come when he would have to meet his enemy, King Ahab, face to face. His training from ravens and a needy widow was only a beginning of his training to be a trusting leader among his people.

But the prophet did not know he would find a secret ally. One of King Ahab's chief overseers, Obadiah, was a loyal worshiper of Yahweh although the king did not know it. Obadiah had hidden away a hundred young Israelite prophets-in-training. He told Elijah the king's plan for Ahab and Obadiah to scout the countryside to see if they could find grass enough near the springs to keep the horses and mules alive for use in King Ahab's army. They would ward off their enemy until the drought would end. This activity would keep the king occupied temporarily. Also Obadiah could use the information to keep the faithful prophets of Yahweh supplied. They and their horses were hidden in a mountain cave.

When Obadiah met Elijah he was both frightened and grateful. They had not met before, but Obadiah recognized the great mountain prophet. He feared for both of their lives at the hand of the king with Jezebel helping him with hundreds of Baal's prophets faithful to her. Obadiah did not know Elijah's plan to allow God's power to work.

Elijah went on with his plan to confront King Ahab with an object lesson to illustrate which deity had power over nature's activity, now in the form of needed rainfall to end the drought.

On Mount Carmel

When, through Obadiah's assistance Elijah faced King Ahab, we read the conditions laid down for the event—a political one in earth's history (18:17-46).

Ahab agreed and the battle at Mt. Carmel was readied. Elijah spoke to all the people in the famous words: "How long will you waver between two opinions? If the Lord is God, follow him; but if Baal is God, follow him" (18:20). But the people said nothing!

Elijah had God's plan in mind. After the prayer of the

450 prophets of Baal produced no rain, Elijah made a like sacrifice and prayers to Yahweh, which were answered affirmatively. (The story may be read in 1 Kings 18:22-40.) The people were convinced Elijah was God's spokesperson, a true prophet and leader.

Then the rains came as Elijah predicted they would. He advised Ahab and his official chariots to flee to Jezreel, the nearest city. In his own ecstasy, Elijah ran ahead "in the power of the Lord."

When Ahab told Jezebel how Elijah had defeated the prophets of Baal, she sent a message to Elijah saying she would have him killed immediately. Elijah was terrified—she was queen and a most powerful one. He fled for his life taking his servant with him. They walked a whole day into the wilderness toward Beersheba.

A Still, Small Voice

Elijah was miserable with depression and prayed that he might die. He lay down under a tree and slept. An angel came with food and drink and awakened him. As a result, Elijah set out on his real journey—to Mt. Sinai, a forty-day walk away but his people's holy mountain. We remember Moses received the Ten Commandments there. Elijah must have hoped to receive directions from the Lord about how to defeat Ahab, Jezebel, and their Baalism. In his depressed state, Elijah lamented to the Lord how faithful as a prophet he had been. "But the people of Israel have broken their covenant with you, torn down your altars, and killed all your prophets," Elijah moaned to the Lord. "I am the only one left—and they are trying to kill me" (19:14, TEV).

But like Job and most other religious leaders, he was really just getting mature to the point at which he could express his real inner self to God—and Yahweh sent a strong object lesson to help him.

A great storm roared through the mountain crags and at its height the Lord instructed Elijah to go out into the storm and face God to hear God's message. First, the Lord passed by and sent a furious wind that split the hills and shattered the rocks. But Elijah heard no message from the Lord.

Then when the wind stopped blowing there was an earthquake. Elijah listened, but he heard no message. Then came a fire but still no message emerged.

After the fire abated and all was quiet, Elijah heard a soft whisper. He knew this was the Lord speaking in the calm. He covered his face with his cloak and went out to stand in front of the cave. "What are you doing here?" God asked (19:13, TEV).

Then he repeated his self-centered prayer with his contention that he was the only true follower of Yahweh left, along with recounting a catalog of people's sins. The Lord told him to go back among the people and enlist others to help him.

The Lord named the official people Elijah was to anoint—Hazael in Damascus as king of Syria, Jehu as king of Israel, and Elisha from Abel Meholah as his own successor as prophet. The Lord said to him, "I will leave seven thousand people alive in Israel who are loyal to me and have not bowed to Baal" (19:18, TEV).

After Elijah had understood God's direction through witnessing the storm, the wind, and the lightning, he realized how like his own methods against Ahab and the Baal prophets all this turmoil was and how ineffective they were. But the Lord was not witnessed in such noisy phenomena of nature.

After the calm, small voice, the Lord's presence and direction became real. Elijah was learning another leadership principle—quiet spiritual resources were available to him that would be more effective than external might.

He also learned that old friends and new converts to Yahweh and thousands of tried and true leaders waited in Damascus to help in God's kingdom work. He went back among the people and found the people the Lord told him awaited his leadership.

One—Elisha—he was especially eager to find. He was to be his successor. He found him plowing in his father's field and went immediately to "cast his mantle upon him" (19:19). They had evidently known and loved each other previously, although Elijah was much older. Elisha disposed of his working share of his wealthy father's estate and went immediately to be the servant in training to Elijah. The mantle Elijah had thrown about his shoulders was the physical means by which the prophetic power was transferred to Elisha (see also 2 Kings 2:1-18).

Elisha continued the revered prophet's work to do away with the Baalites, but he used quite different methods from Elijah. He learned to be friends, not enemies, of the followers of Baal and he led the Israelite kings to do likewise. He was a politician instead of a preacher although he had been granted Elijah's miracle-working power.

B. The Prophet-Leader

by Alvin Lewis

Many people are stunned and startled by the contrasting elements in the personality of the prophet Elijah. For some people Elijah is the most fascinating and forcible figure in the history of Israel. Others rightfully view Elijah as a whirlwind of a personality in the events of ninth-century Hebrew culture. In his overzealousness and enthusiasm for Yahweh, this prophet became a thorn in the flesh for many evil proponents. He had the kind of courage to confront the king and his subjects without regard for his own personal safety.

To the people of his day Elijah, no doubt, represented a rustic, rugged, inflexible champion of God in the spirit of Samuel. At the same time, he possessed the same fierce zeal that characterized Samuel during an earlier era when the nation was developing. With a forthright boldness of heroic proportion, Elijah also deserves the right to be regarded alongside Moses as one of the greatest prophets of the Old Testament. Not to be obscured by time or trouble, Elijah's place in history is vindicated as he appears with Jesus and Moses on the Mountain of Transfiguration (Matt. 17:1-4).

Elijah, then, is the quintessence of all Old Testament prophets in the sense that his life and ministry embody the meaning of prophetic leadership. To qualify as a prophetic leader, according to Elie Wiesel, one must be someone who is searching; someone who is being sought; someone who listens—and someone who is listened to; someone who sees people as they are and as they ought to be; someone who reflects his time, yet lives outside time.[1]

A prophet leader is forever awake, forever alert; the prophet is never indifferent, least of all to injustice, be it human or divine, whenever or wherever it may be found.

God's messenger to all humankind must somehow become the messenger of humanity to God—and herein we find the horns of a dilemma—the more the prophet leader commits his or her life to God, the more he or she becomes an oracle of God. In this dreadful dimensional role the prophetic leader transcends time and space and becomes a link, a bridge, or an instrument in the hands of a just God.

Little is known about the genealogical, social, and religious background of Elijah. We are first introduced to him in 1 Kings 17:1. Where he speaks to King Ahab with prophetic authority and austerity. Despite the lack of historical and personal data about Elijah, the recorded biblical narrative offers much insight into the moods, manners, and motive of this godly leader.

In this chapter I will explore some of the factors and forces that influenced Elijah's role as a prophetic leader. At the same time, I will also examine some of the implications of how Elijah's experiences may apply to Christian leaders who are called to serve today.

Leaders Are Influenced by Their Environment

Whether one accepts or denies the thesis that leadership is fundamentally a function of personality formation and environmental factors, it is still a statement to be reckoned with. Thus, our environment influences the personality, and our personalities may also affect the environment in which we live.

Elijah was a product of the mountainous country known as Gilead and the village of Tishbe. Gilead with its wild rugged terrain lay east of the Jordan River. The people who lived there demonstrated a character like their environment—wild, lawless, uncouth, and unkempt. Most of the inhabitants dwelt in rough stone villages and maintained their existence by keeping sheep.

The glimpses that we draw from the scriptures of Elijah

tell us: he wore a garment made of animal fur with a girdle of leather about his loins (2 Kings 1:8, RSV). No doubt, due to his environment he absorbed into his character an attitude of coarseness and rugged individualism. Thus, we see in his personality a blending of his environment—an environment that helped to shape and develop a personality amid afflictions, hardships, loneliness, stress, and an hostile terrain. This combination of his surroundings, coupled with a strong belief in Yahweh, prepared Elijah for leadership in one of the bleakest periods in the life of Israel.

It would be well if all of us who aspire toward leadership roles would consider the part our environment plays in helping to solidify our leadership style. In no way am I suggesting that we are trapped by our environment, but rather our environment plays a significant role in making us who we are. Therefore, our family, friends, pets, neighborhoods, religious values, and our inheritance of a world view all fashion our personalities and leadership profile.

But we must not just dwell on the physical aspect of the role our environment plays in establishing our leadership potential. It is equally important that we look at Elijah's spiritual environment and keep in mind this was a period of deep darkness, political strife, and religious anarchy. Baal worship had been introduced by Jezebel who had left Tyre to become the consort of the newly crowned King Ahab. Jezebel, with evangelical zeal, moved to establish the worship of Baal and Ashtarte in the vicinity of Jezreel, where she supported 450 priests from her ill-gained revenue. Without a doubt these religious and spiritual conditions played a major part in shaping the values behind Elijah's role as leader. In fact, I believe that as the prophet grew in years he cultivated a strong religious fervor that caused him to feel "very zealous for the Lord God Almighty" (1 Kings 19:14, NIV). Elijah's zeal, mixed with a holy anger, therefore prompted him to move toward spiritual reformation in Israel.

Leaders Are Shaped by Their Experiences

We are the sum total of all we have experienced in life. Some experiences, however, test, traumatize, and turn us in a new direction. Writing about a character like Elijah would be difficult without also describing a few of his experiences. The scripture is quite vivid as we are permitted to peep into the interior of one who experienced such a broad range of moods. As we study the life of this prophetic leader we are able to feel his depression, his burnout, know about his extreme swings of temperament, and affirm the joy he realized as he drew closer to God.

The true value of our experiences are the learnings we are able to gain from them. Admittedly, some do not profit from either the good or the bad experiences we encounter in life. Yet, experiences can become our best teacher about life and living. Consider two important experiences that molded the life of Elijah and laid the foundation he needed to lead Israel.

Only after Elijah had matriculated through two crucial experiences, Cherith and Zarephath, was he able to take on the false prophets of Baal and perform other exploits for God. Cherith and Zarephath are the wilderness and frustration types of experiences that all leaders must pass through, if they are to identify with others, know God more intimately, and discover themselves.

What is ironic in this narrative, however, is that God actually commands Elijah to go and hide for three years at Cherith, shortly after Elijah had appeared before Ahab to tell him that there will be a drought in Israel (17:1-3). But why Cherith and then Zarephath?

Cherith is the place of solitude, searching, and separation. It is that place where we are locked up with God in faith. In like manner Cherith is a place where we experience the mercy and providence of God unfolding in our behalf. Such places are a part of our lives, not because God gets pleasure in seeing us suffer; rather, they are

112

the foundation points that add substance and success to our being. The lessons Elijah learned in Cherith prepared him for later leadership in life. In Cherith he was taught how to rely on God and not himself. Furthermore, he established a bond with God that would later permit him to overcome his most depressing moments. Elijah also learned that his experiences at Cherith were stepping-stones that endowed him to face even more difficult and deplorable conditions (17:2-7).

If there is a lesson to be learned from Elijah's wilderness experience, it is this: Before we are called to go out, we must first go inward. Getting in touch with our own spiritual resources is essential to qualifying as a spiritual leader. F. B. Meyer, in his volume *Great Men of the Bible*, speaks clearly to the meaning of the inward spiritual life. He has this to say:

> The man who is to take a high place before his fellowmen must first take a low place before his God. And there is no better way of bringing a man down than by dropping him suddenly out of an area in which he was beginning to think himself essential, teaching him that he is not at all necessary to God's plan, and compelling him to consider in the sequestered vale of some Cherith how mixed are his motives, and how insignificant his strength.[2]

But Elijah does not stand alone in the service of the solitary life. Moses was alone on the mountain; Isaiah was isolated with God in the temple; Joseph had to face his pit and prison; Jesus experienced the lonely wilderness; Paul spent three years in Arabia. We, too, must discover our wilderness place if we are to model the meaning of prophetic leadership.

All wilderness and solitude experiences are only for a season. Christians are never called to stay in the wilderness to live out the meaning of their lives. So it was with

Elijah. Just as soon as he had settled down to wilderness living, the Lord tapped him on the shoulder and told him it was time to move on (17:8, 9). This time, however, he was told to go and dwell amid strangers and idol worshipers. But it was here that Elijah experienced two great miracles—perpetuating the widow's meal and oil, and raising of the widow's son from death.

Each of these spiritual exploits added immeasurably to his growth and development as a prophetic leader. Zarephath, then, represents Elijah's practicum, which was the outgrowth of the education he received at Cherith. Cherith was a more private and personal experience, while Zarephath was more public and philanthropic. At Cherith he received a relevant spiritual encounter, but at Zarephath he was able to give to the widow and her son food, life, and spiritual nurture. True Christian leaders are those who know how to move in both the spiritual and material realms of life. They know how to be fed by God, and they also know how to feed others.

Dynamic lessons may be learned from these two encounters of Elijah. First, God had a plan for Elijah's life. At Cherith the brook dried up but not the resources or opportunities of God. Dry brooks are always new occasions for service. Second, complete obedience may bring us into a smelting furnace. Literally, the word *Zarephath* means a smelting furnace. It was a city that lay outside the land of Canaan. Many things might have made it unacceptable to the prophet. After all it was part of Sidon—the place from which Jezebel had brought her impious prophets. Notwithstanding the spiritual depravity and the deteriorating environment, the hand of God was still at work. God was at work in behalf of Elijah by providing for him food, shelter, and friendship. And certainly God was at work in the widow's life as he replenished her with oil, meal, the life of her son, and the recognition of Elijah as a true leader and man of God (17:24).

Leaders Must Deal Creatively with Their Emotions

As human beings we sometimes fluctuate between high emotional peaks and the valleys of emotional defeat. The valley experience brings fear, rejection, and low self-esteem. For example, pastors who preach stirring and stimulating sermons on Sunday may suffer from unmerciful melancholy on Monday morning. No less is this true of leaders who build great sanctuaries and Christian education centers, only to find themselves over-stressed, depressed, and victimized by their own success.

In Elijah we have a good case study of a man who had a tough time managing his moods.

The depression and stress that overcame Elijah is something with which every Christian leader should come to grips. None is immune to such stress and depression, and very often depression will attack us when we are at the height of our careers, when we have achieved some outstanding victory or accomplished some worthwhile goal. As we look at other leaders in the Bible we find that they, too, failed just where we would expect them to stand.

Abraham, who was called the father of the faithful, retreated into a compromising lie when he stood before Pharaoh regarding Sarah his wife. Moses failed to enter the Promised Land because he spoke unadvisedly and unwisely to the children of Israel. In the New Testament, Simon Peter, who had walked, talked, eaten, and fellowshiped with Christ, denied him three times before an accusing crowd. If our study of Elijah's leadership says anything significant to us, certainly we may conclude the strong and successful are just as vulnerable to the whims and wiles of emotional attacks as are the weak and unprotected.

But through Elijah's whole ordeal of suffering and despondency, God taught this prophet a valuable lesson about his faithfulness in the midst of an emotional storm.

In spite of the temporary setback, in spite of the depression, in spite of all outward appearances in the land and the people, Elijah learned that God had sovereign control over everything in his world and in his life.

Let us examine several reasons why Elijah failed:

a) Elijah's physical strength had become overtaxed. Think for a moment about the exhausting strain he experienced since leaving the shelter of a quiet and pastoral environment like Cherith and Zarephath. Besides this was the long ordeal of the contest on Mount Carmel with the prophets of Baal; the intensity of his prayer life; the eighteen-mile run in front of Ahab's chariot, followed by a quick flight to the desert. All these consummated in physical depletion. Tired leaders cannot lead—they do not have the stamina or the strength to last. When one is overoccupied and overloaded with his or her own personal and physical problems, it is hard to concentrate on creative matters to lead the people of God and live a balanced life.

b) Elijah felt alone (19:9, 10). One is never alone, however, as long as there is a God who rules the universe. But how easy it is to say and feel, "I only am left." The sad part about repeating and believing such a statement is to accept it as truth. Now there is a vast difference between being alone and experiencing loneliness; for, one can be alone without experiencing loneliness, and one can be in a large crowd and yet be very lonely. At some point and place in his life, Elijah forgot about the one whose presence pervades the universe. He who is omniscient and omnipresent has promised never to leave us or to forsake us.

Someone has well said that it is lonely at the top. What is alluded to in this statement is that leaders must often walk the solitary path. Therefore, a Christian leader may have to, at times, exercise her or his gifts in an atmosphere of isolation away from the crowd. Being alone is a price we sometimes have to pay for our leadership.

116

Nevertheless, it is a worthwhile price to be paid when we realize the benefits to be obtained. Loneliness, on the other hand, is always a state of mind—it is not a state of being. Our loneliness is the result of focusing on our circumstances rather than on God's ability. We need to remember that our circumstances do not dictate our posture or position with regard to who we are and what our relationship to God is. In the midst of our loneliness there is a God who says, "Lo, I am with you always, to the close of the age" (Matt. 28:20, RSV).

Leaders Ought to Lead by Their Example

A leader, says Lloyd Perry, shows the way.

> He directs the course of another by going before or along with the one he is leading. Once a spiritual leader is sure of the will of God, he will go into immediate action regardless of the consequences. The leader knows where he is going and is able to persuade others to go along with him. Leadership is the capacity and the will to rally men and women to a common purpose.[3]

When we view the life of Elijah in the light of Perry's definition of a leader, the prophet Elijah indeed qualifies. That Elijah modeled good leadership by his example few will deny. With his excellent qualities and spiritual example Elijah is uppermost a man of integrity. The word *integrity* relates to a mathematical term *integer*, which is a number that is not divided. This word also carries the connotation of something that is whole. A person of integrity is, therefore, someone who is not divided against himself or herself. A person with integrity does not say one thing and act another way. Thus, he or she is not in conflict with his or her own value system. Jesus was correct when he said, "If a house is divided against itself, that house cannot stand" (Mark 3:25).

117

Because of Elijah's integrity he was able to draw to him an entire school of developing prophets. One of those young prophets he discipled was a man by the name of Elisha. Elisha became Elijah's traveling companion for more than a decade. During that period he had a chance to observe Elijah's behavior, listen to his words, examine his attitudes, analyze his teachings, measure his moods, evaluate his courage, and inspect his leadership. The true measure of any leader may best be understood when one has won the confidence of his followers. One cannot lead if there are no followers, and one cannot properly follow if there are no leaders to model the meaning of godlike leadership.

As the curtain of heaven is about to drop on the life of this prophet-leader, who will soon be transported to the portals of heaven, he extends to his understudy, as it were, a last and final request: "Ask what I shall do for thee, before I be taken away from thee" (2 Kings 2:9, KJV). What an opportunity this was for Elisha and what a gracious spirit on the part of Elijah.

The determined and dedicated Elijah thought, and then spoke, with godlike conviction—"Let a double portion of thy spirit be upon me" (2:9, KJV). Please note, Elijah sought neither wealth nor position nor worldly power nor a share in those things on which he had turned his back when he said farewell to family, friends, and worldly ambitions.

I would hope and pray that those who are called to be Christian leaders can bequeath to others a legacy of spiritual wealth. It is a poor leader who leaves to his followers only the thirst and hunger for more things and stuff of the world. May there be Elijahs in our lives who will have a deep desire to be as we are. Is there anyone who has had a chance to observe your life as a leader and still wants a double portion of your spirit? If not, why not?

As Christian leaders we must always ask ourselves what kind of legacy are we leaving for those who follow our leadership. Have we taught and lived in such a way that others would want to emulate our lives? What do our followers learn when they try to read our lives? Is the quality of the letter they read clear and distinct, or is it blotted and blurred? Do the newly saved have a clearer vision of Christ, or is their opinion of him obscured by what little of him they see written in our lives and attitudes as prophetic leaders?

Notes

1. Elie Wiesel, *Five Biblical Portraits* (London, England: University of Notre Dame Press, 1981), 39.
2. F. B. Meyer, *Great Men of the Bible*, Vol. 2 (Grand Rapids, Mich: Zondervan/Marshall Morgan and Scott, 1982), 70.
3. Lloyd Perry, *Getting the Church on Target* (Chicago, Ill: Moody Press, 1977), 73.

Chapter 8
Ezra and Nehemiah: Teaching and Building Up

A. Ezra and Nehemiah

by Lynn B. Ridenhour

Ezra, Scribe and Governor

Ezra's temporary home was in Babylon where many of the Jews were being held captive. Skillful as a scribe and an interpreter of the Law of Moses, Ezra had become acquainted with the Persian king, Artaxerxes Longimanus. Theirs was a friendly relationship. Ezra longed to return to his home city, Jerusalem, and he asked Artaxerxes if he could take a small group of Israelites remaining in Babylon and go home. Artaxerxes granted his request.

Ezra was delighted and felt he was fulfilling God's purposes. After all, he had prepared his heart to know and do God's will and to teach his people to do the same. Three burning desires of his heart consumed his daily life: First, he sought the law of the Lord by studying and becoming familiar with the sacred writings. Second, he practiced the teachings of God's word in his personal life. Third, he was eager to teach others the Word of the Lord.

King Artaxerxes recognized Ezra's Jehovah as the supreme God, "the God of Heaven." This pleased Ezra. The king's ensuing letter granted much authority and extraordinary powers to Ezra. Among these were permission to take all the people of Israel who wanted to return to Jerusalem and to receive gifts of silver and gold to be used as offerings to God. If Ezra needed anything else for use in temple worship, he was told to take it from the king's treasure house. The king further commanded that anything Ezra felt to be the will of God was to be done.

In addition, Ezra was told to govern the people who returned to Jerusalem. He was granted power to select judges and officials. Authority was given to punish those who disobeyed the law of God or the Persian law. Ezra was even given the right to teach the laws of God to those who did not know them—the Gentiles.

The king showed much confidence in Ezra. He paused to express praise and thanksgiving to God for working through the king's heart. Ezra was convinced that God's hand was upon him strengthening him for a great ministry.

The Journey

Some six or seven thousand persons, many of them women and children, prepared to return with Ezra. This was a much smaller group than the one that had returned with Zerubbabel almost seventy years earlier. The gathered exiles began their journey on the first day of the first month, the beginning of a new year.

After traveling for two weeks, the returning company was camped by the Ahava River. Ezra chose this particular time to inspect the group of returnees closely. He was shocked to learn that no Levites were with them. Ezra immediately sent several of his leaders to a nearby city whose chief leader was Iddo, requesting some ministers for the house of God. The request was granted and forty Levites responded. Ezra gave God the credit: "by the good hand of our God upon us."

Before continuing their journey, Ezra called all the people together for a day of fasting and prayer. Ezra had a feeling that the king would also give them an escort of soldiers for protection if he asked for it. Ezra chose to trust God for safety and protection instead. He and the people prayed for a safe journey protected from thieves.

One final administrative detail remained before the group's departure. Ezra had placed twelve priests in charge of the treasure for the temple. The money was in bullion and needed to be weighed out. The silver and gold vessels were also weighed. Ezra reminded the twelve priests that they were holy men of God and in like manner the silver and gold were holy to God. They were encouraged to be honest in their dealings. (At present-day prices, the gold and silver would have been valued in the millions. A strong guard with an armored car would be required today to transport such a sum through the streets of one of our cities.) Upon completing their four-month journey free from harm, the people gave thanks to God for his merciful care and rested for three days.

Ezra notified the Persian officials and shared the royal decree from King Artaxerxes. They did not oppose the Israelites and in fact they supplied the things needed for temple worship as stipulated by the king.

Trouble in Jerusalem

Ezra had not been in Jerusalem long before he learned of the serious disobedience of the people who lived there. The people had failed to separate themselves from the surrounding nations—Ammon, Egypt, Moab. Even the priests and levites along with other men in the group had married heathen wives. God had chosen the people of Israel to be "the holy seed" set apart to be a people for God's name, but the holy seed had mixed with the idolatrous people of the land.

Ezra was surprised and disappointed, and great was his grief. He began tearing his clothes and pulling out his hair. The tearing of clothes was a common way of showing deep sorrow. The plucking of hair was not so customary. Here was a man with great pangs of grief and much moral indignation.

Ezra sat for hours speechless. How could his people

again turn away from God after God had restored them to their homeland? A group of obedient Israelites gathered around Ezra as he sat mulling over the situation.

Ezra was ashamed of the sins of his people. During the evening sacrifice in the temple court, Ezra knelt before God with outstretched hands and prayed. The entire prayer was a confession of sin; there were no requests of any kind. As a man of God, Ezra identified himself with his people, confessing that "we have forsaken thy commandments." Obviously he was not personally guilty of these sins; however, he spoke as an intercessor for his nation.

Ezra prayed fervently with visible signs of overpowering emotion, "weeping and casting himself down." The news spread quickly. Crowds soon gathered. Ezra's persuasive prayer touched the people and they also began to weep. A man named Shechaniah knew that his father was guilty of the sin Ezra had condemned. He spoke to Ezra offering a remedy: All the people could make a covenant with God to divorce their heathen wives in accordance with the law. Shechaniah's suggestion was accepted.

Immediately Ezra persuaded the priests, Levites, and other Israelites present to promise to do what Shechaniah had suggested. A proclamation was sent throughout the city and province urging all the Israelite men to gather at Jerusalem within three days to make this matter right with God. Failure to attend would result in a penalty: possessions would be confiscated and the person banished from the land. Ezra continued his mourning in secret, fasting from both food and drink. He wanted to know God's purpose and be a true deliverer for the people of God.

The Israelites assembled themselves at the required time. Ezra boldly advised the group to confess their sins and to put away their heathen wives. He further commanded them to "separate from the people of the land." The congregation as a whole promised to do as Ezra asked.

Many hearts ached. Ezra and the elders took three months to review each family situation and handled the matter "decently and in order." Ezra published the list of men who had married heathen wives. Ezra was particularly alarmed that one fourth of the offenders were religious leaders.

Ezra had been a good governor. The people of God had made some spiritual advances. As they realized anew the importance of living lives wholly committed to God, spiritual revival came to God's people.

Nehemiah, Cupbearer to the King

Nehemiah was one of the Babylonian captives who chose to remain in Persia instead of returning to Jerusalem with the liberated exiles. He had assumed a high position in Persia and prospered as cupbearer to the king.

About twelve years passed after the spiritual revival of Ezra. A group of Persian Jews had returned to the palace following a visit to Jerusalem. Among them was Nehemiah's brother Hanani. Nehemiah asked his brother for a report about the people of Judah. He was saddened by the answer that they were "in great affliction and reproach." With the walls still broken, the people were prey to enemies, robbers, and wild beasts.

Nehemiah was so saddened by the bad news that he sat down and wept. For several days he grieved, fasted, and prayed. His reactions were very similar to those of Ezra who had preceded him.

Nehemiah presented his special petition to God in prayer, one of the great prayers of the Bible. He addressed God as one who had uttered many prayers previously and who called himself God's "servant." In his confession of sins and shortcomings as a nation, he said, "We have sinned against thee." Nehemiah deliberately included himself in this confession. He stressed that the Israelites had failed again and again. The people

125

deserved all the trouble that had come upon them, including the captivity. Then Nehemiah reminded the Lord of their covenant relationship, given through Moses, and the promise to regather them in Jerusalem, if they obeyed God's commandments. At the close of this prayer, Nehemiah asked that God would help him to get permission from the king to return to Jerusalem.

Nehemiah Faces a Challenge

There was a task to be completed in Jerusalem. Nehemiah accepted the challenge. Jerusalem was the religious as well as the political center of his nation. He was needed there! The Jews had lost hope, and Nehemiah was challenged to do something about this.

The king sensed the sorrow in Nehemiah's face as he continued his duties at the Babylonian court. When the king wanted to know what was bothering him, Nehemiah again breathed a prayer seeking God's help. According to the court etiquette it was considered rude to be sad in the king's presence. The Persian kings believed that their presence should bring joy and happiness to any person.

Nehemiah asked permission to return to Jerusalem to build up the city and for supplies needed for rebuilding. These requests were granted. Nehemiah, like Ezra, believed this was possible because God's hand was upon him.

Upon reaching Jerusalem, Nehemiah began to survey the ruins at night. Walking around the ruined walls, he sensed the magnitude of the task ahead. Nehemiah counted the cost before beginning, and with God's help determined that he would not quit until the task was completed.

The Jews were urged to "rise up and build." They responded to Nehemiah's contagious spirit. Those who responded were published in an honor roll, a list that included priests, Levites, governors and nobles, businesspeople, youth, and the common rank and file—the whole remnant people.

Nehemiah planned for the people to work where the need was greatest. Work began at the temple in the center and moved out in an orderly manner. Each person had a share in the responsibilities. Various gates were opened up in the rebuilding process. Most persons worked earnestly, following Nehemiah's example, but even while the Tekoite people worked, their leaders shirked their duty.

Opposition Persists

As the work progressed, Sanballat from Samaria and his friends began to ridicule the workers. The sneers turned into threats. Nehemiah gathered his people together and encouraged them as he prayed to God and kept on building. The rebuilding continued because "the people had a mind to work." In spite of difficulties the people had hope of accomplishing their important task and obtaining good favor from God.

A new crisis in opposition from the enemies came when the wall was half completed. Nehemiah learned of a conspiracy to halt any additional building, and he prepared for an attack from outside. Once again, Nehemiah prayed to God. The people set watch day and night and were ready to defend themselves, if necessary.

The Samaritans spread the word that they would secretly attack the Jews and destroy both the people and the wall. Nehemiah reacted by placing guards at strategic points; placing half of his personal servants and bodyguard in work areas and placing swords by the sides of the workers. A trumpeter stood by, ready to sound the alarm if needed. When the attackers saw how well prepared the Israelites were, they called off their plan of destruction.

Another obstacle to the work came from the inside. Some of the rulers were taking advantage of their poor. This angered Nehemiah. He called the rulers together and insisted that they return any property and money they had taken from the poor. Priests were called in to witness promises of the rulers to do as Nehemiah asked. These promises were kept and the quarreling ceased.

The wall was almost completed. Sanballat and his gang once again tried to hinder the completion. This time, Nehemiah was invited to meet with the Samaritans a long distance away to settle their differences. Nehemiah recognized this as a trick to lure him away. Five times Sanballat sent a letter and each time the invitation was refused. Nehemiah could not stop "doing a great work" to talk with them.

The cunning opposition of the enemies failed to stop the Jews. The wall was completed, the gates were attached, and the Gentile opponents were forced to admit that God's blessing was truly on the work of the Jews.

Nehemiah completed this task unscathed because of the quality of his character. Giving God the glory for everything, he revealed the secret of his spirit when he said, "The joy of the Lord is your strength."

Great gladness reigned during the dedication of the wall. Many musical instruments and singers were used in the celebration. The people marched into God's house singing and giving thanks to God, and even the women and children rejoiced with great joy. The joy of Jerusalem could be heard for a long distance. Nehemiah's faith in God, his love of Jerusalem, and his hard work make this possible.

Before returning to Persia, Nehemiah selected persons to rule in his absence. Hanani, his brother, and Hananiah were to be corulers of the temple and the adjoining fortress. Hananiah was selected because he was a faithful, godly man.

Background Notes

Ezra, the Helper: Ezra's name well fits his character, because he was a true helper of God and his own people. Ezra was a priest and a scribe, the first one mentioned in the Bible. As the name indicates, scribes were copyists of the sacred Scriptures. Scribes were also recognized as teachers and authorities on the law—primarily the study and interpretation of the Old Testament.

According to Hebrew tradition, Ezra was high priest of his people before leaving Babylon. In addition tradition gives him credit for collecting the Old Testament books and setting that portion of Scripture in the canon. Ezra was a strong believer in God and God's call upon his life. He often used the phrase "the hand of the Lord was upon me." Some have even referred to Ezra as the "father of preachers." Ezra was the spiritual leader.

Little is known about Ezra's family. He was born during the captivity. His father's name was Seraiah. It is believed that Ezra lived to a ripe old age and died while traveling to the court of Artaxerxes in Persia. It is further believed that Ezra was buried at Samarah on the lower Tigris River. There is no proof that these beliefs are completely accurate.

Nehemiah: The name *Nehemiah* means "Jehovah comforts."Little is known of his family except his father's name Hachaliah, which means "Jehovah is hidden," and a brother named Hanani.

Nehemiah was born during the captivity and became the cupbearer of King Artaxerxes Longimanus, the same monarch referred to in Ezra 7:1. In response to Nehemiah's request, the king made him governor of Judah, a position he held for twelve years. The Bible is silent about the remainder of Nehemiah's life and death.

Nehemiah is recognized as the political leader. Some have referred to him as the "patriot in action."

The books of Ezra and Nehemiah both present plain, straightforward accounts of an important period of Jewish history. Ezra presents the return of God's people from Babylonian captivity and the return of worship in the temple.

Nehemiah presents the rebuilding of the walls of Jerusalem. The word *build* is used twenty-three times, while the words *wall* and *walls* are used thirty-two times.

No other men in the Old Testament have left such continuous narratives of their own deeds and thoughts. Each one tells a story that enables us to trace his endeavors from beginning to end.

Both Ezra and Nehemiah were devout persons of prayer. They sought God's direction before acting. Both realized the need of help from important people in life, but they sought God's help first. They likewise paused to thank God for his answers to their prayers.

Babylonian Captivity: Nebuchadnezzar had taken control of Judah and banished the Israelites from their homeland, placing them in captivity in Babylon. The Jerusalem temple was also destroyed. This captivity lasted seventy years. Nebuchadnezzar took the temple vessels. Cyrus the Great, king of Persia, gained control of the empire from the Aegean Sea to India. He took control of Babylon in 539 BC. Soon after this conquest, God worked through the heart of Cyrus to grant the Jews permission to return to their homeland. He even returned the original temple vessels and commanded the Jews to rebuild their temple.

Zerubbabel ("Seed of Babylon") led the first return of the exiles and rebuilt the temple. The first return was a larger group than the second return with Ezra. The group totaled approximately 31,583 with the number of priests being 4,289. The high priest was Joshua.

B. Teaching and Building Up

by C. Richard Craghead, Jr.

Today's church leaders who face bleak circumstances can find in the stories of Ezra and Nehemiah both encouragement and cautions. Theirs, as is ours today, was a struggle to develop a strong community of faith. Then and now, building up the faith community requires leadership.

The Struggle

We do not have to turn the story of the restoration of Jerusalem into an allegory of today's church in order to see some parallels of common leadership circumstances. Ezra and Nehemiah could have been discouraged by the situations they faced just as an educational leader today can become disheartened in the all-too-typical church scene. When we discover that nearly seventy percent of America's congregations have fewer than a hundred active members, we begin to see what the Jewish priest and the highly capable layperson saw when they arrived in the disheveled city of Jerusalem.

Smaller congregations struggle every week of the year with limited finances, few willing and trained workers, and strained facilities. The educational workers probably feel the burden of these limitations more than the other members of the congregation because their attention is focused on the spiritual growth of the children, youth, or adults they teach. So often they leave the Sunday school hour or Bible study or midweek educational activity and wonder if anything worthwhile was accomplished. These workers can become especially disheartened if, in addition to no words of appreciation, someone rants at them for trying out new ways of teaching or for asking for the switching of classrooms for a learning experiment. Larger congregations also point to strains in finances, faculty, and facilities—just more of it.

Ezra and Nehemiah faced meager circumstances, too. Their toughest enemy was not the marauders or the Samaritans; it was the enemy within the city walls—those who had become content with the desolation of the city for nearly 150 years. Resistance to change, even when those changes might better the lot of the inhabitants, was the major obstacle those leaders faced.

Four Advantages

Ezra and Nehemiah had at least four advantages over the typical educational leader in today's church.

1. *First,* they both had a clear sense of their mission—well, in general terms, anyway. The details of that mission became clearer to them as they began to work at the task each was prepared to perform. Their sensitive hearts prompted them to volunteer to help build up a people who would be obviously faithful to God. The strength of their convictions carried them through rough engagements. Today's educational leaders can learn from their example. When we talk about effective leaders, we must always ask ourselves, What is our reference in measuring effectiveness? If our local setting is like the city Ezra and Nehemiah found, the constituency may say that being effective is maintaining the *status quo.* Fortunately, those two men had some additional advantages in the face of that complacency.

2. Their *second advantage* was that they were from "out of town." They had not grown used to stepping over rubble, hiding when bandits stormed into the city, taking orders from a governor in another city, or looking the other way when coming upon moral and spiritual laxity. Local church leaders need fresh perspectives on their responsibilities and opportunities, too. Leadership periodicals, workshops, conferences, and regular meetings with persons who hold similiar offices in other nearby congregations can often lift the leader to vista points from which the work of the church can be seen more clearly.

3. A *third advantage* held by Ezra and Nehemiah was their commission from the Persian king. They were government officials and had authority to order people around. Of course, such authority is limited to the willingness of those being governed and both leaders had to be careful in how they exercised their authority. Church leaders do not have such authority. No matter how beneficial a program might be, no matter how efficient the congregation may function if certain changes are instituted—today's leader cannot operate by fiat. "Because I said so" is never an adequate reason for directing volunteer members and workers; even if the leader feels that he or she has a mandate directly from God.

Some leaders feel much frustration from the need to communicate clearly with their constituents while seeking to gain mutual "ownership" of the task or project. Ezra and Nehemiah could have destroyed their assignments if they had chosen to rely only upon their kingly authority, but they were wise enough to realize that willing cooperation of the Jerusalem residents was the only way to make progress toward their goal.

4. Their *fourth advantage* may be shared by many of today's church leaders. Ezra and Nehemiah were more interested in being faithful than in being popular. They chose what we might call a conservative route to reach their goal and laid foundations that affected Jewish faith and practice for generations. They called for changes that would make the Jerusalem inhabitants stand out from their neighbors, changes that would show an obvious fidelity to God. Their demands cost money, embarrassed some social relationships, and even disrupted family life. None of this made these two persons popular, but by the grace of God, reform and renewal did come.

Now for a Look at the Cautions

Those same four advantages suggest cautions for church leaders today. The four can be grouped into two pairs of issues. That Ezra and Nehemiah were from out of town and had the endorsement of the Persian king suggest the issue of power. That both men had a clear sense of mission and were committed to faithfulness and not popularity speaks of purpose. Let us look first at purpose.

Leading with a Purpose

The story of Ezra and Nehemiah reveals the necessity of an inclusive purpose in the church ministry. Together and individually those men were concerned for both the physical and spiritual well-being of their people. At first Nehemiah seemed most intent on reconstructing the walls around Jerusalem to protect its inhabitants from both harassment and perversion. When he returned to the city a few years later, he discovered that the walls did not protect the people from their own inner contaminations. He then set up a series of reforms that would help the people recognize themselves to be part of God's story of salvation. For them that meant getting rid of Tobiah, the scoffing Samaritan who had been allowed to take up sumptuous quarters in the temple precincts, establishing a tithing system to support the functions of the temple servants, observing the Sabbath as a day of worship and rest, and refraining from any more marriages between Jews and non-Jews.

Ezra worked hard at setting up practices that had been found helpful in keeping the exiled Jews mindful of their covenant relationship with God. Thus, his reforms helped the people to discover their own common story and to discover both their heritage and their destiny under God. By giving new meaning to feasts, circumcision, and Sabbath-keeping, he pointed to meanings beyond mere commemorating of nature cycles. He brought the reading of the Law into the common practices of the people. The word of the Lord told them of their selection by God and deliverance from Egyptian slavery. The reading reminded them of the covenant that would make them both blessed and a blessing.

Today's church leader with any experience knows that vitality drains away from any congregation that loses its sense of purpose. When only confusion answers a central question of life—Why are we here?—the congregation wanders aimlessly, somewhat as the Apostle Paul wrote, "Blown here and there by every wind of teaching and by the cunning and craftiness of men in their deceitful scheming" (Eph. 4:14, NIV). That had already been happening to those left behind in Jerusalem, and Nehemiah and Ezra worked to build up their core of identity as God's chosen people.

Church leaders share that task today. All of us need tangible evidence in our daily lives of the identity we claim by faith in Christ. Therefore, leaders are wise who help congregations set up practices that spring from and point to their sense of calling from God. A primary task of any church leadership is helping the congregation to articulate for itself its godly vocation and to evaluate periodically how true to that mission is the congregation's work and witness. Occasionally the declaration of mission the congregation has formed needs to be adjusted because experience and resources have changed since the mission declaration was first composed.

Ezra and Nehemiah worked with the Jerusalem leaders to draw the city's people into their true identity. Gaining a clear sense of mission may be as difficult in the local church as it was for those two leaders who faced terrific resistance from the very ones they were trying to serve, but such is the bedrock on which all other aspects of congregational life is built. In at least two ways, however, we will want to move beyond the examples of Ezra and Nehemiah.

First, we no longer want to wall ourselves off by social norms and exclusiveness from our neighbors. Christ has made clear that the gospel is for all people, everywhere, and God's people are now to go into all the world with the good news. God loves every person, sinner and saint alike. Our leadership task today is to gain for ourselves and those we serve a sense of ministry that includes both those within our local fellowship and those "to the uttermost parts of the earth." Therefore, our second concern is related to a global sense of mission. Part of our leadership task is to build up persons who can dialogue with unbelievers, not shun them. If we can do this, we can admire the model of Ezra and Nehemiah without having to follow every detail of the mode or intention of their story.

The Right Use of Power

As was mentioned before, Ezra and Nehemiah were government officials and had the power of the Persian king authorizing their work. They could command people to do their bidding. That same authorization probably protected them from direct interference from the Samaritan governor and others who would have preferred to keep Jerusalem in a weakened, vulnerable condition. Reading their story may influence today's church leaders to think that they, too, may operate as though they have the power to command. But two other factors may be overlooked when noting the exercise of power by those reformers.

1. First, both men were well off, probably wealthy, and certainly quite respected in Babylonian exile. They had reached positions of considerable esteem. Nevertheless, they were willing to give up their comfort to travel over dangerous miles and into unfavorable conditions to be of service to those who were suffering both terrors and deprivation. We must admire them for joining the lot of

the people of their country back home in Jerusalem. Their willingness to risk themselves probably lent a credence to their instructions that was not ignored by those who might otherwise have distrusted them. There was a consistency in their message. They were not like those who say, "Do as I say, not as I do." They practiced what they preached, as the old saying goes. That is a good lesson for today's church leader. He or she who shows by participation that the work and circumstances of team members are understood will be received with a much higher degree of cooperation than the one who directs from the sidelines.

2. A second feature of the power of leadership given by Ezra and Nehemiah is seen in how thoroughly each of them did his homework. Notice that Nehemiah, for instance, did not arrive in Jerusalem and start yelling orders in all directions, even though he could probably see a hundred jobs that needed to be done as soon as he stepped through the broken walls. Instead, he took a few men with him and toured at night the walls of the city, taking at every step notes of the chores that had been waiting for generations. When he did lay out his plan, it was thorough and well explained. Detractors were disarmed by Nehemiah's familiarity with the Jerusalem situation, while supporters were probably delighted to find that their hopes for renewal were not misplaced. Today's leaders could take a lesson from Nehemiah: "Do your homework!"

3. Of equal importance is the willingness of both men to allow the principle of the mustard seed to work. They wanted their work to last, and that would occur only if the people could claim in their hearts the significance of the rebuilding and the reforms. Thus, both began their respective tasks with a small team of those who shared something of their vision and who were willing to let that vision grow. Then each leader engaged all ages and

groups in the work, worship, and celebrations to the point where the whole community felt the strength of what they were doing together. As the years went by, less and less was the community divided into "them and us" companies. This did not happen overnight, but it did happen because Ezra and Nehemiah relied more on motivation than coercion.

In summary, the lessons for today's leadership in the church can be seen in the following features of the leadership styles of Ezra and Nehemiah. First, they worked from the sure conviction of God's calling, what we can call a sense of mission for today. Second, they shared the power that was theirs with the people they had elected to serve, reminding us that Jesus told his disciples that they were not to lord it over one another, but to be servants of one another.

Chapter 9
Daniel: Daring to be a Leader

A. Daniel

by John E. Stanley

An old chorus challenges us to "Dare to Be a Daniel." Leaders who learn from Daniel will develop a public faith rooted in God's authority but tested by the counsel of trusted peers. Modern Daniels will confront problems. They will communicate contemporary Christian meanings by seeking a usable past within their inherited traditions. Chapter 2 of the Book of Daniel demonstrates Daniel's leadership.

The narratives in Daniel 1-6 show how some Jews emerged as leaders in the courts of foreign kings. In the court tale contained in Daniel 2, Daniel's ability to interpret vision led King Nebuchadnezzar of Babylon to recognize Daniel as a leader.

Nebuchadnezzar's troublesome dreams produced insomnia and mental anguish. To find relief, Nebuchadnezzar summoned would-be interpreters to tell him what he had dreamed. He promised the Chaldean interpreters riches and honor if they could state the meaning of his dream. The king, however, upped the ante by threatening to destroy the magicians, enchanters, and sorcerers if they could not interpret the dream. At this point the Babylonian interpreters asked the king a second time to tell them his dream, but Nebuchadnezzar accused them of stalling and threatened them with dire consequences

139

if they did not get busy with his request. Realizing the impossibility of their situation, the Chaldeans answered the king, "We cannot explain a dream that you have not shared with us. Only the gods can do such a feat."

The king's anger exploded. He decreed that "all the wise men of Babylon be destroyed" (Daniel 2:12, RSV). The executioners included Daniel and his companions in the death threat. Rather than passively accepting his fate, however, Daniel questioned Arioch, the king's captain, saying, "Why is the decree of the king so severe?" (Daniel 2:15). When he heard about the king's plight, Daniel made an appointment with Nebuchadnezzar to interpret his dream.

But Daniel was not a Lone Ranger as a leader. Instead of trying to discover the dream by himself, he gathered his three companions together to pray. The four Jews confessed to each other that they did not want to perish with the rest of the wise men of Babylon. At this point their Jewish necks were lying on Nebuchadnezzar's chopping block just as were the heads of the Babylonian sorcerers. At night God provided Daniel with the solution. Daniel responded by blessing God in a prayer, thanking him for providing wisdom, strength, and the answer to the king's mystery.

After a season of prayer Daniel informed Arioch, "Bring me in before the king and I will show the king the interpretation" (Daniel 2:24).

In a rush, Arioch brought Daniel to the king. For the first time Arioch distinguished Daniel from the Chaldean wise men by identifying Daniel as an exile from Judah. The king asked Daniel if he could recite the dream. In quiet confidence, the Jewish exile assured the Babylonian monarch, "No person can describe or explain your dream. But the God in heaven has revealed to me the mysteries you seek to understand."

Daniel stated (vv. 31-35) and interpreted (vv. 36-45) the dream. He began his dream report with a direct address to Nebuchadnezzar: "You saw, O King." Then Daniel described an image with a gold head, silver breast and arms, bronze belly and thighs, and iron legs with feet of iron mixed with clay. A stone of nonhuman origin struck the image and the four metals were broken into pieces. Even while the wind blew the broken pieces about like chaff, the stone became a great mountain and filled the earth.

Daniel's interpretation paralleled the dream report. Again he addressed the king directly (vv. 36-37). Daniel identified the metallic body parts as four successive world kingdoms beginning with Nebuchadnezzar. The fourth kingdom of iron will crush the previous dominions. Because iron mixed with clay becomes brittle, however, the fourth kingdom will not endure. Just as a stone of nonhuman origin smashed the metallic body parts in the dream report, Daniel announced that God will set up a dominion that will break and surpass the four world monarchies. With assurance Daniel concluded the dream interpretation, "The dream is certain, and its interpretation sure" (v. 45).

Verses 46-49 describe Nebuchadnezzar's positive response to Daniel's feat. The king prostrated himself in humility before the Jewish exile. He acknowledged Daniel's God as "God of gods and Lord of kings." He bestowed gifts on Daniel and appointed him as ruler over Babylon and chief supervisor over the wise men of Babylon. The tale concludes with Daniel leading the king's court. Nebuchadnezzar, king of Babylon, designated Daniel, a Jewish exile, as a court leader because Daniel delivered on his promise to describe and interpret the king's dream.

Background

Court tale and apocalyptic vision. The court tale and apocalyptic vision seen in Daniel 2 introduces the two main types of literature in the book of Daniel. These literary forms serve the purpose of announcing to readers that God intends for Jews to be faithful while they serve under foreign rulers even as God prepares a future kingdom for the saints of God.

Jews preserved and told court tales to instruct Jews how to survive and be faithful when ruled by Gentile kings. When Daniel's life was threatened because Arioch counted him among the interpreters of Babylon (vv. 12-13), Daniel's devotion to the Hebrew God (vv. 17-23) enabled him to triumph in his contest with King Nebuchadnezzar. Daniel's fidelity and feats led the king to acknowledge Daniel's God as "God of gods and Lord of kings." Daniel's rise to leadership in the court tale of Daniel 2:1-30, 46-49 is paralleled by the court tale of Esther and the saga of Joseph.

An apocalyptic vision, another literary form, is a revelation regarding the future in story form. The vision comes from a heavenly sender to a human recipient. An apocalyptic vision, the Book of Revelation for example, provides a people in stress with a hope of relief because the vision promises the imminent advent of a heavenly intervener.

These two literary forms, court tale and apocalyptic vision, in Daniel 2 introduce the two main types of literature in the Book of Daniel.

Daniel as a figure of wisdom. The author of the book described Daniel as "skillful in all wisdom, endowed with knowledge, understanding learning" (1:4). Daniel's wisdom surpassed that of Babylonian wisdom figures (1:20). Daniel demonstrated his wisdom by interpreting dreams (2:31-45; 4:1-27) and by deciphering a writing on a wall (5:1-28).

Wisdom in the Book of Daniel differs somewhat from the wisdom of Proverbs. In Proverbs wisdom is the skill of knowing how to live by basing life on respect for God and the Law. In Daniel, wisdom includes being faithful to Jewish traditions (1:8) and involves skill in remembering visions and dreams. In addition, wisdom entails reflection upon the meaning of writings that eventually became accepted as scripture such as Jeremiah 25 (see Dan. 9:2-27). After the Exile, a group of learned interpreters of Jewish traditions and writings emerged. They became known as the *hasidim*. Daniel 11:33-34 probably refers to these scribes.

Although Jewish tradition, Matthew, and at least one Dead Sea scroll text speak of Daniel as a prophet, Daniel appears to have been simultaneously a prophet and a figure of wisdom. Prophets and wisdom leaders were not necessarily exclusive or separate categories of leaders in the second century BCE. Daniel received revelation directly from God and also as he reflected on Israel's traditions and writings.

Daniel 2 discloses that figures of wisdom were plentiful as evidenced by Nebuchadnezzar's summoning of them. Also, Daniel 2:48 mentions wise men. Thus, being a wisdom leader did not in itself constitute Daniel's significance. What distinguished Daniel from others was the source of his wisdom: God (2:20-23). Daniel's faithful use of wisdom led a foreign king to acknowledge Daniel's God as supreme. Daniel's fidelity inspired other Jews to be faithful to Jewish tradition while under the yoke of oppression.

The symbol of four world empires. What is the historical meaning of the symbol of four world empires? While I am aware that different interpretations of this symbol exist, I understand the symbol to represent four monarchies in Daniel as follows: gold, representing the Babylonian; silver, Medean; bronze, Persian; mixed iron and clay, Greek/Hellenistic. The best argument for this conclusion comes from internal evidence within the Book of Daniel. The organization and structure of the book identifies the four world monarchies. Consider the trail of evidence Daniel has left.

The author places chapters 1-4 during the reign of Nebuchadnezzar of Babylon. Belshazzar, whom Daniel calls a Chaldean king, steps into Daniel's drama in chapter 5. The Chaldeans were the last phase of the Babylonian Empire. Darius the Mede (5:31—6:28) and Cyrus of Persia (6:28) represent the second and third empires. The Hellenistic kingdom of Greece was the fourth kingdom. The reference to "mixed marriages" (2:40-43) probably refers to the political marriages arranged between Egypt and Syrian/Greek rulers to cement their alliance in 252 BCE. In Daniel 7-12, the same four kingdoms appear. Belshazzar of Babylon (7:1; 8:1), Darius the Mede (9:1), and Cyrus of Persia (10:1) reign. In chapters 7-12, as in chapters 1-6, the fourth kingdom is the Greek empire symbolized by "the little horn" or King Antiochus I of Syria, which was a Greek state (7:7, 11, 19-26). In summary, the four world empires are Babylon, Medea, Persia, and Greece.

The meaning of the symbol arises not from the first four empires but from the fifth! Daniel opposes foreign rule. He proclaims that the four world dynasties will be followed by a kingdom established by God. To a people experiencing the loss of kingship and an eroding faith, Daniel promises a sovereignty established by God whose rule shall never be given to another people (2:44). The symbol of four world empires called Jews to resist accommodating their loyalty to God to the values of a ruling culture.

B. Daring to be a Leader

by John E. Stanley

Involvement in the Issues of the Day

Daniel's faith was a public faith in the political arena. A leader involved in the political and intellectual struggles of his day, Daniel served as an adviser of foreign kings. No one who has read the symbol of four world empires in Daniel 2 and 7 can legitimately say that faith does not involve political dimensions.

This book is written in memory of Don Courtney whose involvement in the affairs of his city I admired. He was a Christian and a church leader who saw the need to take his faith to the Rotary Club, the public school system, and the Madison County Cancer Society. Daniel demonstrates that effective Christian leaders will become involved in the public sphere.

Daniel submitted to divine authority and challenged inadequate human authorities. The sources of leadership for Daniel were God and the counsel of trusted peers. Daniel 1:8 defines Daniel as a person who dared to disobey the king's orders. Likewise, the examples of Shadrach, Meshach, and Abednego document the heroic witness of Jews who refused to accept the decrees of pagan Babylonian culture. These four leaders found ultimate authority in God, but they prayed and reasoned together to test the legitimacy of what they perceived as the call to follow a divine drummer. Leadership for Daniel came from God and was shared with his three wise counselors. Daniel's leadership became designated influence because of his institutional office after Nebuchadnezzar appointed him to an official position.

Human authority is necessary. Civil authority in political and social institutions prevents chaos and can protect individuals. We live in an era, however, when Christians are too often asked to submit unquestionably to human authorities. Inadequate leaders frequently encourage us not to rock the boat. We are told to fit in and to get along with the system. Seldom are we asked to change a system that squeaks.

Two recent presidents—Lyndon Johnson and Richard Nixon—tried to suppress dissent by religious leaders who opposed their political policies. Some Christians feel paralyzed unless they are covered by a cloak of pastoral and male authority. Sometimes senior pastors act more like the military commanders of staff ministers than like team leaders. Prominent voices continue to make money preaching a false gospel of submission to an authoritative chain of command. These are only a few signs that indicate how persons are pressured to conform and to submit to authorities.

A button on my office wall reminds me to "Question Authority." I believe authority should be questioned in a respectful and reverential manner. If the authority appears legitimate after being questioned, then it should be accepted. Daniel documents that we are first to be faithful to God. And fidelity to God sometimes requires us to question would-be human authorities.

Sometimes pastors as leaders must challenge the inherited authority of lay persons who function as church bosses. As a pastor Don Courtney questioned the authority of my great-uncle who was the church treasurer. Don suggested that the ninety minute worship service be shortened to seventy-five minutes so that Sunday school could be lengthened from thirty to forty-five minutes. My uncle threatened to leave the church if Sunday school was lengthened at the expense of worship. Quietly but confidently Don challenged the authority of this church boss and Sunday school was extended to forty-five minutes. My uncle left the congregation for fifteen years.

Sometimes pastors must be challenged because they are abusing authority. An incident from the life of Mary

Cole illustrates this truth. Mary Cole was a Church of God evangelist around 1900. Some women came to Mary Cole saying, "Sister Cole, we have come to the conclusion that we won't testify to sanctification this year, lest we offend the minister. He does not want us to testify."

Sister Cole responded, "If a minister is going to oppose sanctification so much the more will I testify to it throughout the year." Sometimes truth leads us to challenge religious leaders.

As a young minister I occasionally sought the counsel of Don Courtney. At one point some church leaders were pressuring me to quit pushing for change in a sensitive area. I believed I was serving the broader church and God by challenging what I felt to be injustice. I shared my feelings of loneliness with Don. He counseled, "John, you must pray and decide what is right. Then follow where you understand right to be. Obey God and your conscience." Later I learned Don agreed with and worked for the position I advocated. But before he told me where he stood, he asked me to clarify what authority I was following.

The church needs leaders who are not blind followers. We need ministers and laypersons who dare to ask if a new program is only a fashionable fad or a significant trend. Leaders ask questions and seek answers. Leaders envision diverse ways of accomplishing tasks rather than thinking there is only one way to address a problem. Daniel dared to be out of step with foreign kings and compromising Jews because his ultimate loyalty was to God and what he perceived to be right.

From Death to Life

Daniel transformed suffering and death into reasons for survival. Evidence abounds that Daniel's community experienced persecution and suffering (Daniel 3; 7:7, 21, 23-26). Reflecting on how his community was responding to persecution, Daniel saw that some Jews were forsaking their faith to escape stress (11:32, 34). Other Jews resorted to armed military resistance as the Maccabees died in 164-163 BCE. Rejecting apostasy and armed resistance as viable options, Daniel called the saints to wait for God's fifth world monarchy, a kingdom given to the saints of the Most High (2:44-45; 7:27). Daniel anticipated the demise of the mighty fourth world kingdom and called the saints to stand firm amid persecution and stress. Daniel transformed their crisis into a reason for living.

Although Daniel addressed a corporate struggle for life against death, his truth applies on the personal level. I remember the afternoon in 1986 when Hollis Pistole told me that Don Courtney had a fast-growing malignancy. Hollis and I were attending Chicago Theological Seminary, and so I did not see Don until he was home recuperating from surgery. Only time would tell if the surgeons had excised all the cancer. Watching him find the will to live in his initial struggle against cancer helped me to face up to the threatening feelings I experienced in seeing him ill. His illness was only the second time when a loved one of mine was threatened at an early age by death. His courage taught me about life as he confronted death. Leaders help persons transform problems into opportunities and crises into reasons for living.

Using Tradition Well

As a wise leader Daniel discovered a usable past in the traditions he inherited. Daniel was schooled in Jewish wisdom. He studied and interpreted sacred texts such as Jeremiah 25. Daniel even reinterpreted the symbol of four world empires. In Daniel 2 the symbol uses four metals to represent four human dominions whereas in chapter 7 the author of Daniel casts the symbol in terms of four beasts. In Daniel 2 the symbol seems to resist Hellenism in general whereas in Daniel 7 the symbol resists the specific evil King Antiochus IV. During a time of social stress due to the religious and intellectual competition posed by the attractive lure of Greek civilization, Daniel knew that if the Greeks continued to convince wavering Jews that Greece was the legitimate God-ordained fourth world kingdom, then many Jews would leave Judaism for Greek ways. Therefore, Daniel studied Jewish texts and traditions from the past. He sought new meanings in old symbols. Living in the second century BCE. Daniel was fortunate that the teachings of Israel's main prophets and historians were then in written form. As a wise leader Daniel studied these sacred texts and traditions. As he pondered the past in light of the new challenge posed by Greek civilization Daniel did not throw out his inherited faith. He did not dilute Judaism to make it compatible with the new era. In fact Daniel reached back into the prophetic faith of Judaism and rediscovered in Jeremiah, Isaiah 40-66, and Ezekiel a theology that affirmed God's eventual intervention in history. Daniel found the taproot of his apocalyptic theology in the coming together of Jewish wisdom and prophetic traditions. A new cultural challenge forced Daniel to rediscover the prophetic faith of Israel.

Contemporary leaders would be well advised to study as Daniel did. We need to find contemporary meanings in the texts and traditions we have inherited. But I suspect not enough persons are doing that. I once served on the pulpit committee of my congregation. I listened to many sermon tapes from prospective pastoral candidates. Most candidates did well in telling what the Bible says. Their sermons were full of biblical language. But very few candidates took the biblical truths and packaged ancient ideas in contemporary illustrations and applications. These potential leaders failed to do what Daniel did so well. Daniel knew how to find a usable past for the emerging future. As a leader he was a step ahead of the crowd.

A humanism that seeks to order life without any reference to a divine transcendent dimension is the contemporary parallel to the Greek culture of Daniel's day. Effective Christian leaders will not confront the current challenge of humanism by diluting Christianity. Instead we should restudy our holiness heritage and the Bible and show that, like humanism, the holiness tradition stresses the potential goodness of persons. We emphasize human possibility rather than human perversity. But our accent on human potential comes because of the power of the Holy Spirit as sanctifier. Like humanism, we can be hopeful regarding the future. Yet the Christian hope is a resurrection hope born in the grace of Christ. Our realistic hope remembers how cruel the twentieth century has been. We recall the concentration camps, the bombings of Hiroshima and Nagasaki, the widening gap between the affluent and the poor, and the refugees and famines we have created.

We can hope for a better future because we know God has given us the freedom to build tomorrow from the choices we make today. We believe history has a final purpose and meaning just as God imparted a purpose to life in creation. To the lonely in our success-oriented society we offer the church as a community of Christian love where persons can find a sense of belonging and becoming. Our mission requires us to discover the best truths and practices we have inherited and then to offer these to a world longing for religious faith even as it tries to organize life without reference to God. As Daniel found a usable past adequate for the crisis of his time, so can we as leaders find a usable past in our holiness heritage.

Dare to be a Daniel! His public faith was rooted in God's authority and shared with peers. Through his study he transformed problems into reasons for living. By finding a usable past in his religious tradition, he was a leader who was a step ahead of the crowd.

Chapter 10
Jesus: The Inner Side of Leadership

A. Jesus

by Kenneth G. Prunty

A Young Boy Leads the Way

Curious and excited about the trip to the feast of the Passover, Jesus could hardly wait until the caravan arrived in Jerusalem. He was twelve years old and curious as he could be. How many people would be there? Who would he meet? What would they talk about? Within an hour after the group arrived, Jesus was meeting people, talking about the Romans, and discussing religion. Jesus was up for a good time, and the whole adventure was off to a good start. He was especially intrigued by the conversations in the temple. Any discussion about the kingdom of God involved Jesus in deep thought and caused him to do his best and deepest thinking.

The temple discussions were so intriguing that Jesus did not notice when his parents and the whole caravan headed out of Jerusalem. To complicate matters further, his parents did not realize that he was still in Jerusalem. Thinking he was elsewhere in the traveling group, they didn't worry about him. But before long they wondered about him and began trying to find him. His mother and father were dismayed when they could not locate him.

Much worried, they returned to Jerusalem. After three days of frantic searching, they found him in the temple, "sitting among the teachers, listening to them and asking them questions" (Luke 2:46, RSV). Mary and Joseph were impressed by what they heard about him and excited and surprised when they realized that "all who heard him were amazed at his understanding and his answers" (v. 47).

"Son," his mother blurted, "why have you treated us so? Your father and I have been searching anxiously for you."

Jesus' response to their anxious questions gave them little comfort. "How is it that you sought me?" Jesus wanted to know. "Did you not know that I must be in my Father's house?" (v. 49). Mary and Joseph could not make sense out of Jesus' new independence and assertiveness. "Who does Jesus think he is?" they wondered. "Is he seeing himself as a temple leader?" His parents were greatly puzzled.

As they prepared again to leave Jerusalem, Jesus seemed ready to go. He returned to Nazareth with them.

Though Mary and Joseph and the community did not understand Jesus' actions in Jerusalem, they were impressed with the many positive signs of healthy growth. "Jesus increased in wisdom and in stature, and in favor with God and man" (v. 52). It was clear to all who were close to Jesus that when there is a balance of inner wisdom, sound physical growth, deep faith and closeness to God, caring relationships and open communication with people, greater maturity and service can be expected.

Unusually perceptive, Jesus sensed that his life might be uniquely challenging. Sometimes lying in the shade of a sycamore tree, he could see himself on a busy path talking with people about life and how it could be happier.

As he mingled with community and temple leaders and talked with uncles and aunts and grandparents at family gatherings, Jesus sensed a special destiny about his life. Though not fully aware of who he was or what he would become and do, he knew intuitively that his life would not be average or normal. Throughout his younger years, Jesus talked with community and temple leaders. He tried out his ideas on any group of people who would listen. When people would argue with him, raise questions, and doubt what he was saying, Jesus was especially challenged. These times were not always pleasant, but deep inside he liked these times best of all. When challenged, he had to think again and again. He would study the scriptures and hear the stories as they were told by the rabbis.

When Jesus was about thirty, his leadership and ministry became active and fully realized (3:23).

Leadership Calls for Vision!

One day when Jesus was traveling alone in Jordan, he wandered deep into the wilderness. Deep in thought and troubled in spirit about his life, he was consumed by searching questions that struck at the center of his being. There he was tempted and tried for forty days (4:2). The agony was devastating. Every facet of his being was tested. Something of a vision quest, this time in solitude, enabled Jesus to seek vision and wisdom, courage and confidence for his life.

Unlike one modern political leader whose face, *Newsweek* stated, "appears not to have been lived in," Jesus came out of the wilderness with a face lined with character and a countenance emulating courage. Jesus had confronted the depths of life spiritually, politically, and socially. The vision that emerged from the wilderness journey provided Jesus a powerful image of his ministry and leadership. This he confessed in the synagogue in Nazareth where he had been brought up:

"The Spirit of the Lord is upon me, because he has anointed me to preach good news to the poor. He has sent me to proclaim release to the captives and recovering of sight to the blind, to set at liberty those who are

oppressed, to proclaim the acceptable year of the Lord"
(4:18-19, RSV).

First Servant, Second Leader

This vision confirmed Jesus as first a servant and second
a leader. He would always let his leadership grow out of
his servanthood. Though Jesus' first acts of leadership
brought the kind of acceptance and acclaim that effective
leadership needs, he had earned both through devoted
service to the powerless. Jesus was clearly first a servant,
second a leader. He had learned to be leader by first
learning to be servant. Radically, Jesus clearly demonstrates that servanthood is the way his followers are to
become leaders. He had come "down the up staircase"
to lead his people!

When Jesus called his first disciples to follow after him,
his leadership entered a new phase. It is one thing to
astonish your friends and family with what you do and
say. It is quite another challenge to meet with others and
invite them to join you in a common mission. The vision
and endeavor were the kingdom of God.

The Gospel of Mark gives us an instant replay of the
calling of the first disciples. "When Jesus was walking
along by the Sea of Galilee, he saw Simon and his
brother Andrew casting a net in the lake, for they were
fishermen. 'Come, follow me,' Jesus said, 'and I will
make you fishers of men.' And at once they left their
nets and followed him. When he had gone a little
farther, he saw James, son of Zebedee and his brother
John in a boat, preparing their nets. Without delay he
called them and they left their father Zebedee in the
boat with the hired men and followed him" (Mark 1:16-
20, NIV).

The next day again John was standing with two of his
disciples; and he looked at Jesus as he walked, and said,
"Behold, the Lamb of God!" The two disciples heard
him say this, and they followed Jesus. Jesus turned, and

saw them following, and said to them, "What do you seek?" And they said to him, "Rabbi [which means Teacher], where are you staying?" He said to them, "Come and see." They came and saw where he was staying; and they stayed with him that day, for it was about the tenth hour (John 1:35-39, RSV).

In these word pictures, we see Jesus' sense of his own reality, of his own being, and how it impressed those he met. The quality of his leadership called persons who met him to "follow after him."

No Followers, No Leaders!

Jesus possessed the stature to lead others, to call persons to follow after him. Jesus, as with all leaders, faced the question about whether or not he could empower others to share and carry out his dream. Could he share his leadership with others?

Jesus was a sensitive leader who loved people and sensed their deepest needs and values. Many people listened to Jesus and were drawn to him. Jesus referred to some of these as his disciples. They carried a special loyalty and devotion to Jesus and what he said and did. Some were called specifically, and these Jesus called his disciples, companions, or his friends. Others Jesus called more generally. Jesus cared about these followers immensely but recognized that those he needed to share his leadership must carry a deeper devotion.

Jesus carefully observed these disciples who were seriously interested in being close to him. He knew that people who got close to him would catch his dream. "Which of these," Jesus wondered, "can be trusted with the keys to the kingdom?" He pondered for days about which of these he could most fully share kingdom leadership. Whom could he empower to be his disciples? With whom could he share leadership most deeply? Who could in fact become apostles?

Any organization with leadership so shortsighted as to

be concerned with only the present moment is destined to extinction. Jesus felt challenged by the future of the kingdom of God. Choosing those persons with whom he would share his leadership was the most important leadership decision he had to make. For this decision he needed deep insight and wisdom.

When Jesus "went up into the hills and summoned those he wanted," he was making a strategic decision, a decision whose consequences could not be changed easily. So those whom Jesus summoned came to him and from them he appointed twelve. They were to be his companions and to be sent out to preach, with power to cast out devils (Mark 3:13-15).

These companions, these leaders with whom he was sharing the kingdom dream, needed to be intelligent, thinking, committed persons, fully trustworthy. These leaders were to be perceptive and possess wisdom. Jesus said loudly: "If you have ears, then hear." Jesus explained, "Hear more than my word, understand the meanings, see the images of what I am saying."

Jesus had no intention of plunging his hearers, his followers, into hopeless confusion. He often told his disciples stories with vital below-the-surface meanings. He wanted to make them think and wanted to show them how. His aim for his disciples was to shock them out of being spectators, to make them abandon any intellectual short cuts, and to get them to work hard at the only thing that mattered: building the kingdom of God.

Jesus Sought Thinking Followers!

Committed to help people think and to go on thinking until they found what was right, Jesus lived with his disciples, sharing his thinking with them at the deepest level possible. What was right, of course, was the reality of the kingdom of God.

One day Jesus got into a boat, and his disciples followed him. As the boat sailed toward the middle of the lake, a terrible storm swamped the boat with waves. To the dismay of the disciples, Jesus was asleep. They awakened him with their cries for help.

The storm diminished as Jesus spoke, and there was a great calm. The disciples were puzzled and impressed with Jesus' ability to quiet the storm on the lake and in them. They also in this experience felt more confident about their decision to follow him.

How to Be a Great Leader

As he walked and talked with his followers, Jesus exercised a variety of fruits of leadership. He was gentle with children and with the poor and powerless. He was strong and sometimes autocratic with those in power. His courage, his wisdom, his timing, his flexibility, his caring for the kingdom of God and for people, and his sharing of leadership enabled him to be influential and effective in a variety of situations.

Now when Jesus noticed the great crowds of people all around him, he gave orders to go over to the other side. A scribe shouted, "Teacher, I will follow you wherever you go." The scribe was dismayed and surprised when Jesus responded. "Foxes have holes, and birds of the air have nests; but the Son of man has nowhere to lay his head" (Matt. 8:19-20, RSV).

Jesus' leadership was beginning to show its shape more clearly. He made uncompromisingly clear to his disciples that to follow him required a commitment with little room for other interests. Another disciple after indicating that he was ready to go, said, "Lord, let me first go and bury my father." The disciple was greatly confused and discouraged when Jesus said to him, "Follow me, and leave the dead to bury their own dead" (vv. 21-22).

"Leave the dead to bury the dead?" the man questioned to himself. "Jesus, you have to be kidding. My grandfather, my father, and everyone I have ever known have always buried the dead." He struggled in his mind about what Jesus could possibly be doing. Jesus asked for a break with the past, and it was painful. Jesus was a leader who had high expectations of those who would follow after him.

As is true with all great leadership, the courage of one's convictions was essential for Jesus. One day just before the Passover, we see Jesus on his way up to Jerusalem.

> In the Temple he found people selling cattle and sheep and doves, and the money changers sitting there. Making a whip out of cord, he drove them all out of the Temple, sheep and cattle as well, scattered the money changers' coins, knocked their tables over and said to the dove sellers, 'Take all this out of here and stop using my Father's house as a market.'
> —John 2:13-17, JB

Everybody in the temple that day who wondered about the leadership of Jesus and whether or not he could stand up against injustice around him, saw their questions fade into the shadows. All in the temple saw strong leadership come forward from Jesus when the situation demanded it. The children, the poor, and those who questioned the authority of the temple priests and the Romans realized Jesus possessed strength of character.

Another picture of Jesus' leadership is seen in his reaction to the request of the mother of the sons of Zebedee for them to receive special places of honor. Jesus almost whispered as he called the disciples and their mother close to him. "You know that the rulers of the Gentiles lord it over them, and their great men exercise authority over them." He leaned close to them as he said with confidence, "It shall not be so among you; but whoever would be great among you must be

158

your servant, and whoever would be first among you must be your slave" (Matt. 20:25-27, RSV).

Jesus Not a "Lone Ranger"

If Jesus' leadership is primarily the result of divine intervention and blessing, should he be able to function easily in solo, "Lone Ranger" fashion as a leader? One day while he was speaking to the people, his mother and brothers stood outside. When told of their presence, Jesus responded with surprising words. "Who is my mother, and who are my brothers?" And stretching out his hand toward his disciples, he said, "Here are my mother and my brothers! For whoever does the will of my Father in heaven is my brother, and sister, and mother" (12:46-50, RSV).

In an instant Jesus made it clear that he was not the "Long Ranger." He was a leader in community. He was a leader in concert with those who believe in him and who are committed to his ways. Participation with him and his participation with his followers was unquestionably his style of leadership.

A Model of Servant Leadership

No greater model of servant leadership exists than the picture of Jesus washing the feet of his disciples. To the great amazement of all, Jesus "rose from supper, laid aside his garments, and girded himself with a towel. Then he poured water into a basin, and began to wash the disciples' feet, and to wipe them with the towel with which he was girded" (John 13:4-5, RSV).

When he had washed their feet, and taken his garments, and resumed his place, he said to them, "Do you know what I have done to you? You call me Teacher and Lord . . . for so I am. If I then, your Lord and Teacher, have washed your feet, you also ought to wash one another's feet. For I have given you an example, that you also should do as I have done to you. . . . I say to you, a servant is not greater than his master; nor is he who is sent greater than he who sent him" (vv. 12-16).

In this simple act Jesus demonstrates that serving comes before leading. To be a leader is first and foremost to be a trusted servant. If we are first leaders and second servants, we get lost in our leadership and cannot follow in the spirit of Jesus' leadership. Leadership demands servanthood first!

We Learn about Leadership from Jesus

To consider the leadership of Jesus from a human point of view is both challenging and enlightening. It is easy and possibly simpler to think that all of Jesus' leadership was divinely given. If that view is fully accepted, we will learn less from Jesus about our own leadership. If, however, we recognize that Jesus learned about leadership from being a child of his parents, a student of Jewish rabbis and teachers, a citizen of a country dominated by a militaristic Roman regime, a student of human behavior and reflective of his own leadership, then there are few limitations to what we can learn about leadership by observing his leadership and his life.

It is helpful also to remember that Jesus was one of several religious leaders in the territory of Galilee who called persons as followers. Galilee was a small territory some fifty miles long and twenty-five miles across. Galilee was not noted for its religious soundness, and yet it produced many sages before, during, and after Jesus' lifetime. Something about Jesus' thinking, his vision of life, his message, and his style of leadership made him unique. Jesus' sensitivity to the influence of his leadership was often revealed as he asked, "Who do people say that I am?"

In this question Jesus was in a sense checking to see how his leadership was being perceived. He knew there are no leaders without followers and what followers believe about leaders greatly affects how leaders lead. Jesus also knew that who he was in the minds of the people was expressed by their responses to the "who do people say that I am?" question. The dynamics of the relationship between leader and follower was understood and appreciated by Jesus.

Jesus was a determined leader whose very character was like granite. He was at times compassionate and tender and at other times furious with the *status quo*. The poor and the powerless stirred the deepest mercy in him. The rich and the powerful religious could arouse his consternation and anger.

When dealing with the powerless, he was usually the "gentle shepherd." In confronting the powerful he could be dynamic and autocratic. Jesus was an excellent model of what Kenneth Blanchard and others today would call a "situational leader." Jesus could be and in fact became the kind of leader the situation demanded.

Servant leadership for Jesus was the willingness and the ability to serve in whatever ways necessary to accomplish the mission, the kingdom of God. Jesus' all consuming leadership task was to bring in the kingdom of God, to establish it on the face of the earth.

Jesus believed with deep conviction that he was the central figure through whom God's purposes were to be fulfilled. When the people around him could not see or understand his mission and worse, rejected it, Jesus was not only troubled and dismayed but uneasy and angry. The acceptance of the kingdom of God as a desirable reality was so important to Jesus that its rejection was beyond his understanding. Seeking first the kingdom of God was the foremost task of believing in his leadership and following it.

How Jesus the servant leader went about carrying out his leadership is our central concern. What we can learn for our own leadership is an important second concern. No greater model of true servant leadership can be found in human history!

B. The Inner Side of Leadership

by Kenneth G. Prunty

"And now here is my secret, a very simple secret: It is only with the heart that one can see rightly; what is essential is invisible to the eye."

—The fox to the little prince in
The Little Prince by Antoine de Saint Exupery

Tuning into the leadership of Jesus asks us to dig beneath the surface of Jesus' deeds and leadership behavior. It pushes us to ask about more than what others thought of him or about how he appeared to others. Seeing the leadership of Jesus asks us to get behind his eyes and inside his skin to consider his consciousness.

What goes on inside the leader is a most significant factor in all leadership. Leadership is from the inside out more than from the outside in. How a person sees himself or herself influences how others are seen. What you say to yourself, what you tell yourself about yourself, about others, and the world around you determines to a great extent the quality and style of your leadership.

We would like to understand more about Jesus' leadership than what the evangelists wrote about him in the New Testament, yet these are our only sources of information. Jesus' leadership grew from his inner consciousness, as does all leadership. It is the inner side of leadership that we must come to understand in Jesus if we are to learn and understand his leadership for ourselves. We will seek to understand Jesus' leadership from several perspectives.

Two significant dynamics are involved whenever leadership is exercised.

1. The first is what goes on between leaders and followers, the group leader and group members. We have some good pictures of this dynamic of Jesus' leadership

from the New Testament. We have read many articles, heard numerous sermons, and studied and prepared dozens of Sunday school lessons. Yet all of this may have given us a somewhat distorted image of Jesus and the kind and quality of leadership he exercised.

2. The second is what goes on inside the leaders. The inner person of the leader, the hidden self, is the most important dynamic in any leadership transaction or activity. We have few glimpses of the inner leadership in Jesus and all other leaders we have known. This is the part of leadership that is most unknown and least understood by all of us. It is the dynamic of leadership that is most difficult to sense. It is also the piece of leadership development for which we get the least help.

Leadership is essentially invisible! It is spirit. Its dynamics are not discernible by the physical senses. This is what makes it both so difficult and so important. A renewed interest in the care and feeding of the hidden self, the inner self, is long overdue. The physical body is important but cannot be more than a body without a healthy inner self. Strengthening the inner muscles of the hidden self is a strong focus here. Only as the hidden self grows strong can effective inner leadership develop. The real you is invisible. What is essential about you and me is invisible to the human eye. That is both our problem and our opportunity.

No one in history has been more sensitive to the importance of the inner self than Jesus. He recognized that this inner, hidden self has the ability to be reflective and contemplative. These are essential skills for all effective leadership. To be able to step back and see oneself gives anyone's leadership a second chance to be caring and sharing. To stop and think, to act and then reflect, to get outside one's behavior, and to see oneself as if another person looking on is necessary to all good leadership. It is the hidden self that is able to do this.

Jesus realized that if the hidden self is weak and

undernourished or so unconscious that self-awareness is lacking, contemplation and reflection are impossible. There is good reason for us to look more closely at the leadership of Jesus. No greater example of caring leadership coming from the inner self has ever been lived.

The Basis for Jesus' Leadership

For much of human history, most people believed that only certain people were born to be leaders. The kings and queens were born to be kings and queens, and the rest of us were born to be their subjects. Persons were born to be generals and presidents and all others were to be the soldiers and the common citizens. Only in recent generations has there come to be a widely held belief that all persons can be leaders. We are not born leaders. We are made leaders.

But how about Jesus? Was Jesus born to be a leader? From all that we can read in the scripture, Jesus was born into this world with a very special mission that assumed leadership. So in Jesus' case, can we say he was born to be a leader? The answer seems to be a strong yes.

How did Jesus learn to be a leader? Was Jesus born with the vision for leadership and all of the skills he needed to be an effective leader? The answer appears here to be no. Jesus learned basic leadership skills from his family and community like everyone else. Each of us is given gifts and abilities, and some of those gifts make certain kinds of leadership a greater possibility. Yet what we do with our gifts and abilities is a far more important issue than the specific nature of the gifts.

Furthermore, everyone who has any influence with another person is a leader. With that definition of leadership in mind, let's turn it around and say that we are all born to be leaders. Some of us, with the gifts we have been given and the opportunities we have had to appreciate and learn to use our gifts, carry greater leadership responsibilities than others. Jesus wanted all persons to be fully human in their own right and to exercise the leadership and discipleship they had discovered.

It is always difficult for the followers of Jesus to see him as a human being, as a gifted leader of the people of his time for the cause of the kingdom of God. As Jesus accepted the special mission given him by God the father and exercised the gifts given to him, his calling to leadership became clear. The effectiveness of his leadership grew through study, observation, and modeling.

What Is Jesus' Leadership Style?

To be a leader is one thing. To be a particular kind of leader is another. Leadership style has to do with what a person does as a leader. How does a person view herself or himself? How are other persons seen? What is the person's view of the world? Who is God and how is God understood?

A leader can be the big boss. Or could be the organization man or woman. Or could be an easy going, placating kind of person who seldom takes action. Some leaders are more democratic, seeking the wide participation and involvement of everyone. Still others are "servant leaders" who can be whatever kind of leader the situation calls for.

What kind of leader is Jesus? Jesus was seldom the "big boss." In driving the money changers out of the temple and in the way he talked to the religious leaders of his day, he certainly carried out an autocratic leader style. But he had no great control needs that drove him always to be in charge.

Jesus in no way was like Diotrephes, who is vividly described in 3 John 9 as one who liked to be in charge and put himself first. Rather Jesus often put himself last and only took charge of situations reluctantly when there was no other way.

In Matthew 8:18 we read about Jesus asking his disciples to go with him to the other side of the lake. In the storm they encounter, Jesus asserts the confidence of his leadership by staying relaxed. His friends realize how dependent they are on him and feel afraid for their safety when they notice he is relaxed and sleeping. He was comfortable and assumed his disciples would feel secure in seeing him so confident and relaxed. He would desire not to take charge of the situation but let the influence of his leadership be felt in his quietness. When he asked why they were afraid, feelings of disappointment and anger are evident.

Leadership studies now indicate that much of our leadership styles grow out of our own value systems. Autocratic, big-boss style leaders who lead in this way most of the time usually do so out of their own insecurities and lack of skill. Often we behave autocratically because we are afraid of someone else taking charge and because we do not know what else to do. Abraham Maslow reminds us, "When a hammer is your only tool, everything looks like a nail."

There are of course times and situations when autocratic leadership is appropriate. In situations of great danger such as a burning building or a hurricane or tornado, someone who can see what to do rightfully tells others what to do and how to do it. Sometimes in the church persons who are totally dominated by an autocratic spouse or a big-boss type in the workplace come into the church situation ready and willing to take charge. They have been bossed around and now look for someone or something to boss around.

Robert Greenleaf, Jr., in his classic book *Servant Leadership* urges adults who are committed to servanthood and servant leadership simply to refuse to follow any leader whose style of leadership is not servant leadership. The goal of every servant leader is to enable all persons to grow and mature in Christ and to empower them to become their own person in the community of faith and love.

As we all grow up in every way to be more like Christ

we are less open to be bossed around. When we are no longer babes in Christ and we are becoming more mature disciples, we are not satisfied to be treated like ignorant waifs by leaders who have not noticed how much we have matured. Jesus knew his followers and disciples. As they became more fully his companions, he moved from calling them servants to calling them friends. Jesus knew the wisdom of leadership that does not need to be highly visible to be effective. He trusted the relationships with his friends, and he felt comfortable calling them by name in the most friendly way possible.

Jesus' total commitment to servant leadership is most visible in the beautiful act of washing the feet of his friends. In Jesus we discover that when we in fact serve each other, we earn the right of leadership. In the Christian community, no leadership worthy of Jesus Christ can be other than that of servanthood.

How Did Jesus Function as a Leader?

In many ways Jesus in all of his kindness was a demanding leader. In his words, "Let the dead bury the dead," Jesus asks for total commitment, a parting from the past (Matt. 8:21-22). Jesus demands total freedom from the family for the disciples. Hardly one saying of Jesus runs more sharply counter to law, piety, and custom than do these words. This relentless hardness on Jesus' part as he calls his disciples reveals the unconditional nature of following him. This call of discipleship cannot be understood as part of the effectiveness of Jesus as a "teacher." It can be explained only on the basis of his unique proclamation of the imminent kingdom of God. The kingdom was so important that it demanded total commitment, a seeking first above all else, if it was to be realized.

This severe calling of his disciples meant that Jesus gathered around himself a circle of adherents of his own. Jesus' leadership and influence were so strong that it was not necessary for him to demand a regulated life-style for his disciples that would distinguish them from the public. To be his disciple calls for unconditional commitment, a commitment that shaped inner attitudes and influenced outer behavior. Yet Jesus does not make this discipleship a condition for salvation nor does he make his followers into a sect. The discipleship came as a result of seeking first the kingdom of God and of opening that kingdom to all who would believe and follow after him.

Jesus did not wish to train his followers—like the rabbis—to be 'disciples' later so that in a sense they would take the place of the master as teachers. He called them and us to discipleship now, to seek first the kingdom of God today.

What Leadership Skills Does Jesus Emphasize?

What characteristics of leadership are exhibited here and how do you evaluate them? What skills did Jesus use in his leadership? How did Jesus learn these skills in home/family, synagogue, community? What did Jesus believe and assume to be true, and how did these beliefs and assumptions affect his leadership?

The leadership of Jesus cannot be understood except in community. Leadership for Jesus and in all leadership texts today is a dynamic interaction growing out of a loving and caring community. Dale Oldham, well-known Church of God preacher and songwriter in the middle years of the twentieth century, wrote a song generally titled in our hymnals "Let Me See Jesus Only." This title suggests that relationships with Jesus are one on one. Apparently Dale Oldham was troubled about the title and in a camp meeting sermon in the 1970s revealed that he actually wanted the song titled, "Let Us See Jesus Only." The "us-ness" of leaders and followers is caught up in this title. A sense of community that characterized the leadership of Jesus.

"Following Jesus" means in the deepest biblical sense an unconditional sharing of the master's destiny. This sharing includes deprivation and suffering with the master and demands complete trust on the part of the person who "follows." A follower of Jesus has placed his destiny and his future in his master's hands. Jesus called his disciples to participate in his mission and authority and to share his cup toward the dawn of the complete rule of God.

What Distinctives in Leadership Does Jesus Offer?

Louis Rial, founder of the province of Manitoba in Canada in 1885, declared with great certainty, "Yes, during my lifetime I aim at practical results. After my death I hope my spirit will bring practical results."

Jesus hoped for a different kind of results in his lifetime, and after his death, he gave his spirit to his followers so that they with him could bring about practical results. No human life approaches the vision and quality of life exemplified in Jesus and made possible in human situations by the Holy Spirit after Jesus' death and resurrection.

There was once a farmer, who, through careful planning and hard work, had created an unusually beautiful and well contoured farm. One day a superpious friend came to visit. As they traveled about the farm, the visitor kept saying, "My! Isn't it wonderful what God can do!" He said this several times much to the chagrin of his farmer friend. Finally after hearing the words one more time, the farmer in disgust replied, "Yes, it is wonderful what God can do! But you should have seen this place when God was taking care of it by himself."

Jesus offers to us a model of a living partnership with God, our Father. In his leadership we have a beautiful example of a leader living close to his Creator and to his followers. Through such rapport with his followers and intimacy with creation and the Creator, Jesus could lead.

He paced his disciples, knowing how they perceived life. From having walked in their shoes, he could lead them into fresh new paths.

The Lord and leader of our lives calls us to walk in each other's shoes and to be in harmony with life and the giver of life. As leaders we are called to a living partnership with the Leader of leaders. These are the sources that give our leadership effectiveness.

Chapter 11
Stephen and Philip:
Servant Leadership

A. Stephen and Philip

by John L. Albright

Stephen and Philip were two of the seven chosen by the Christian disciples at Jerusalem to administer the charities of the church. The church early felt its obligation to help the poor and needy, and as often happens with this kind of benevolence some complained of being treated unfairly. Some of the Christians of Greek background complained that their widows and other needy ones were frequently overlooked in the distribution of charitable offerings in favor of the needy who were Jewish Christians. The apostles felt that they needed to give full attention to their special ministries of preaching and prayer and could not give adequate consideration to the debate being raised by the complainers. Therefore, they instructed the disciples at Jerusalem to appoint seven qualified persons to administer this special ministry. Often these seven are referred to as deacons, but that name is not ascribed to them in the Book of Acts. The fame of two of them has received immortality— Stephen, the first Christian martyr, and Philip, the evangelist.

Stephen

If you were to visit the National Gallery in London you could see one of Rembrandt's self-portraits. It is considered a masterpiece. Would that each of us could see herself or himself in this light. Clarence E. Macartney in his book *The Wisest Fool* reminds us that we all have the potential to produce a masterpiece of self.

> Day and night, year in and year out, in conscious and unconscious moments, his words and deeds, his secret desires, what he permits or refuses, every hope, every fear, every purpose—all are strokes of the brush, and produce the painting. One day the canvas is finished. Death frames it and puts it on exhibition. Then not a line can be erased or changed, not a feature retouched or altered. The work is finished. There is a masterpiece, a masterpiece because it is absolutely true to life.*

Is There an Angel in Each of Us?

Acts 6:15 tells us that as Stephen sat before the Sanhedrin, his face was seen by the council as the face of an angel. What a tribute coming from those who wanted to kill him! Imagine the impression Stephen must have felt when those who stoned him heard him pray that this sin not be held against them. His enemies had been looking for a traitor, a blasphemer, but instead they saw the face of an angel—a masterpiece for all to see.

Stephen had come to be known as an effective proclaimer of the Good News. His enemies decided to put a stop to his preaching. They brought him before the Sanhedrin with trumped-up charge of blasphemy against the law of Moses. In a memorable and lengthy self-defense, occupying the seventh chapter of Acts, Stephen denounced the charges and those who resisted the truth and sought to slay him. A verdict of guilty found the angry mob dragging him outside the city where he was stoned to death. In verse 59 we have this footnote to the account: "The witnesses left their cloaks in charge of a young man named Saul."

At least three unusual thoughts come to our attention as we read of the martyrdom of Stephen.

1. *First,* other than the crucifixion of Jesus, this is the only death in the Bible that is related with any degree of detail. Most of the closest followers of Jesus fade from the scene of the New Testament without a mention of how they died. One exception is that Acts tells us that Herod killed James, the brother of John with a sword. But Stephen's death is presented with an item-by-item account.

2. A *second* unusual aspect of this remarkable story is the beautiful prayer Stephen made in behalf of his murderers even as he was dying. Throughout church history not a few leaders have thought this prayer was used by the Holy Spirit as a means to convict Paul.

3. *Third* and perhaps the most striking incident of this story is what is indicated of Stephen when he was arraigned before the Sanhedrin. The council, as they all sat looking directly at him, "saw that his face looked like the face of an angel." While the biblical account indicates that this occurred at his trial, we might wonder if it did not also happen at his stoning. As Stephen prayed, each person, if not actually seeing his face again in such a manner, would surely have vividly recalled his appearance earlier in the court room. As he "saw Jesus" his face must have shown with a brilliance reminiscent of the earlier scene. Could it be that this was the look that plagued Paul; the look that convicted him and eventually led to his conversion?

In this beautiful story we have presented to us our own Christlike potential. Stephen, only human, showed his finest hour when he prayed for his murderers, even as Christ had done before. The cross awakens in each of us a sensitivity to its message. It presents life's greatest opportunity for receiving and giving love. As our Lord set the examples, and as Stephen responded in like manner, so also may all believers follow in the manner that best glorifies God. Likely that response will not lead to sacrificial death, but if so, the faithful follower is ready.

Faith Conquers Fear

What might we say prompted Stephen to such heroic, Christlike behavior? Stephen was the first Christian martyr. It would seem reasonable to feel that he was inspired and strengthened by faith. That statement makes little sense to the doubter, and certainly faith is difficult, if not impossible, to explain rationally, but another believer another person of faith can come to accept how the faith of Stephen could support him and give him wisdom and courage in such a moment. He saw Jesus. His faith lifted him up, and he caught the reflection of the glory that is in the face of Jesus Christ.

Faith lifts us to our highest and reveals us at our greatest. We are created to see more than can naturally be seen, and to reach farther than the outstretched hand can reach. God has given much natural potential to each of us. But only as we reach to a power beyond ourselves, to the one who gave us potential in the first place, can we realize all that is possible for us. For the Christian, faith is the reason for any worthwhile accomplishment. Faith is what keeps us in touch with God, and we know that apart from God, anything we do is worth nothing. "In him we live and move and have our being" (Acts 17:28). That can only be understood through faith. We can undergo major losses in life, but not the loss of faith, for it is faith that sees us through our losses. If our faith fails us, all is lost.

The Courage to Do

Can you think of anything more noteworthy than the courage required for Stephen to take his solitary stand for Christ and the church? Stephen alone stands against the powers, against those who would seek to destroy the early church. He takes center stage to present his case, and so capably did he do it that it was recorded for all history to take notice.

Stephen could have taken the easy way out; he could have offered some dull, trite remarks. He could have stated that his trial was a matter of misinterpretation. Rather, he stood in the historic line of prophets, those to whom he referred in his defense as spokespersons for God. He proclaimed the truth of the God of all the faithful prophets and declared the members of the Sanhedrin as betrayers and murderers of Jesus. What an example after which all believers since may pattern themselves.

The Greatest of These

Faith and courage are wonderful attributes, but they are not sufficient for Stephen to have faced what he did. Something more was necessary, and that was love. He had to love a cause, to believe in a cause before faith and courage could carry him. That cause for Stephen was Christ, and the person of faith understands that Christ represents the greatest cause of history—the sacrificial death of God's Son so that we might know salvation.

Stephen's love is manifested in another way. He denounced his enemies and his murderers for their hardness of heart, for their persecution of the prophets, and for their persecution and crucifixion of Christ. But we see no malice or vengeance in his heart. While suffering the physical pain of dying, and enduring the hatred and humiliation directed at him, he prayed that his sufferings not be held against his accusers—those who actually threw the rocks. He wanted them relieved and saved from that judgment. Only love can help one reach that state of spiritual quality, of forgiveness. Jesus admonished us to love our enemies, bless those that curse us, do good to those who hate us, and pray for those who despitefully use us and persecute us, that we might be children of our God who is in heaven. Stephen's wonderful forgiving spirit lifted him to that level.

Stephen was a good and devout man. To his enemies he was a mere human being; one who could and should be disposed of, in hopes that his death would also put an end to the infant church. What they did not account for was the depth of his goodness and devoutness. While breathing his last, through faith, courage, and love, Stephen was able to look to Jesus and see the glory of God—and by his example all since have been able, through faith, also to see the glory of God. As a result, the flames of the early church were not extinguished but only fanned to burn brighter. Paul could not at the time see that glory. Later he did, and since, millions have witnessed to the glory of God who can live within us.

Philip

James Morgan, an aspiring professional hockey player who was known as much for his ability to swing his fists as he was to swing his hockey stick, was once asked if he would prefer his epitaph to read James Morgan the fighter or James Morgan the man. His response: James Morgan the hockey player.

How would you like to be remembered? How would I? We are not always in control of how we are known. Philip would likely be pleased, for he has been known as the evangelist. The book of Acts names him that: "We reached Caesarea and stayed at the home of Philip the evangelist" (Acts 21:8).

Philip the evangelist is not to be confused with the Philip who was one of the apostles. This Philip, as stated earlier, was one of the seven chosen by the Christian disciples at Jerusalem to administer the charities of the church. Stephen, the first Christian martyr, was also numbered among the seven.

After Stephen's death an intense persecution was waged against the Christians at Jerusalem. The chief persecutor was Saul of Tarsus, whom we observed earlier was the one who watched the coats of those who stoned Stephen. While the apostles themselves remained in Jerusalem, many of the believers left to escape the persecution. Those who scattered "went everywhere declaring the word." It is worthy of mention that the wrath of the enemies served a good purpose, for the message of Good News was rapidly spread about. The persecution that was intended to destroy the infant church only served to strengthen it. God is never ultimately defeated, and those who faithfully serve share in God's victory.

Philip's First Missionary Journey

As he fled Jerusalem, Philip the evangelist traveled to Samaria, and there he preached the gospel. That may sound like a very ordinary happening, but be reminded of the alienation between the Jews of Jerusalem and the people of Samaria. The Samaritans were a mixture of Jews from the north kingdom of Israel and the heathen from Babylon, who had been brought in to settle the land by Sargon when Samaria was captured and its citizens had been led into captivity. They embraced some expectation of a Messiah and practiced some sacred rites and rituals of their own. Though they had erected a temple on Mount Gerizim, they were considered with the utmost contempt by the Jews.

In the parable of the Good Samaritan, Jesus stressed that the third person to pass by the injured and the one who stopped to help was a Samaritan. This was the last person a Jew would have attributed characteristics of love, caring, and a faith that would be exercised in such a way. Do you remember when Jesus talked with the woman at the well of Samaria—that woman, married five times, and of "unsavory reputation?" She was amazed that Jesus would converse with her. From this we get

179

some idea of how completely devoted Philip was to the teachings of Jesus, how overwhelmed he was by the love that Jesus had demonstrated. In loving response, he followed the example of his Savior. Acts 8:8 informs us that there was great joy in Samaria because evil spirits were cast out, paralytics and cripples were healed. This is an indication of the power of the proclaimed Word when presented with the blessing of the Holy Spirit.

Philip Encounters the Eunuch

Philip's obedience was tested when through an angel of the Lord he was instructed to leave populous Samaria and go into the desert country to the South of Gaza. Why? Had he not done God's work adequately, and had he not enjoyed much success as a preacher of the gospel in Samaria? We know that he brought joy to so many people. But he put self aside, obeyed God and set out for another mission field. John and Peter, having heard of Philip's work in Samaria, and having traveled there to learn about it, were left in charge of all that Philip had begun. Likely Philip felt troubled for leaving.

At an intersection of a road from Samaria and one from Jerusalem, Philip met an Ethiopian, the treasurer of Queen Candance of Ethiopia. The distinguished man was returning from a visit to Jerusalem, his purpose not being financial or political but religious. Bear in mind that he had traveled some twelve hundred miles through lands known for religious emphasis. Now, returning from Jerusalem, he possessed a copy of the Scriptures, books now found in our Old Testament.

Different theories have been advanced regarding how this Ethiopian would be interested in the worship of Jehovah. Possibly a traveling Jewish merchant had introduced him to this way of thinking and worship. Or perhaps, as many Ethiopians would have it, Menelik, the son of the Queen of Sheba and of King Solomon, was the link with the Jews. We cannot be sure, but it is recorded that this man had learned of Moses and the Jewish sacred Scriptures.

Sensing the leading of the Holy Spirit, Philip went near the Ethiopian's chariot. Imagine the regalness of the chariot and the mighty Arabian steeds. Much courage was required of Philip to do this. The visitor was reading from Isaiah 53 that beautiful passage, "Who has believed our message and to whom has the arm of the Lord been revealed? . . . he was led like a lamb to the slaughter, and as a sheep before her shearers is silent, so he did not open his mouth" (vv. 1-7). As was customary, he was reading aloud. Philip interrupted asking if he understood what he was reading. "How can I . . . unless someone explains it to me?" (Acts 8:31).

The Ethiopian eunuch then invited Philip to come up and sit with him. He asked Philip to explain what he had been reading. "Then Philip began with that very passage of Scripture and told him the good news about Jesus" (v. 35).

Today, we can record great messages. Would it not be a treat if we had an accurate account of Philip's inspired message? The Ethiopian believed and desired baptism, and so the chariot was stopped and the two went into a nearby stream. How fulfilled Philip must have felt to lead so notable a person to this moment of commitment to Jesus. We are told the Ethiopian went on his way rejoicing and we assume to witness to the Savior to whom Philip had introduced him.

The Evangelist and the Missionary

A third noteworthy event occurred some twenty years later at Caesarea, on the coast. Paul was on one of his missionary journeys at which time he would end in Jerusalem where unfortunate circumstances would meet him. He stopped in Caeserea and stayed many days with Philip. Notice that Philip, who had left Jerusalem because of the persecution headed by Paul, was now yoked

181

together with Paul in common ministry for their Savior. We can only imagine the bond both felt as each related his ministry—the joys, the sorrows, the victories. How pleasant it would have been to eat, pray, and swap humorous stories and friendship with these two great leaders of our Christian heritage.

We learn also that Philip led his children in the faith, for he had four virgin daughters who gave themselves to the work of God. After that meeting with Paul, we no longer hear of Philip the evangelist in deed, but his contribution is long remembered. Philip was not an apostle, not an ordained minister as we would think of professional church leadership today. He was chosen by the apostles, however, to do a work of charity for the church, and he was chosen by the Holy Spirit to be a special messenger. As a lay member he responded, and his work is recorded as among the greatest. He served effectively where he felt led in his individual search for God's guidance, and this in concert with the wishes of the church.

Notes

*Clarence E. Macartney, *The Wisest Fool* (Nashville: Abingdon Cokesbury, 1949), 132.

B. Servant Leadership

by Betty Jo Hutchison

Do servant leaders serve by leading or lead by serving? The words *servant* and *leader* have been paired so frequently that we have come to think of them as inseparable. Although the pairing of these words certainly expresses Jesus' one nonnegotiable qualification for leadership, we have used the words with enough repetition that their deeper meaning has become clouded in generality. Reading again the stories from Acts of Stephen and Philip will allow us to look through the window of scripture at two who are remembered because they led by serving.

Of course one could argue that the answer to the question above is both! Some who have leadership positions through election, appointment, succession, or volunteering express their servanthood through leading. In the truest sense it seems that those whose primary motive is to serve come to be known as leaders who make a difference. Stephen and Philip were appointed by the apostles to serve. We have no record of how long they continued the assignment of assisting with the needy, but we see in each of the experiences that followed the Christlike qualities of servanthood.

Servant Leaders Express Internal Consistency

There is a congruity in this leader's life between what the person is and what the person says or does. Stephen and Philip were identified by the apostles as two who could attach the practical hands-and-feet ministries to the gospel message of loving service. They could lead in such a way that all persons, regardless of role or status, would feel supported, rise to higher stature, or become achievers.

Servant Leaders Lead from Within

The disciples were instructed to choose seven men who "are known to be full of the Spirit and wisdom," for the responsibility of carrying out the service ministries of the church. Stephen is described as "a man full of faith and of the Holy Spirit," and again as "a man full of God's grace and power"—and in Philip's encounter with the Ethiopian, he responded to the prompting from "an angel of the Lord" and "the Spirit."

Servant leaders possess inner poise that invites trust and confidence. Servant leadership is often perceived as an intuitive leadership. It cannot be precisely defined or described in lists of actions or outlines of assignments or accomplishments. In Milton's poetic phrase, "They also serve who only stand and wait." Servant leaders convince by their presence. Stephen and Philip's first assignment was to "wait tables"—not a position to be sought for title or authority! But we can be certain that even in this first assigned task, they became recognized as men filled with God's grace and the Spirit of powerful love.

Servant Leaders Are Disciplined

Servant leadership is exacting. It calls for hard work, tough-mindedness, wisdom, and discipline, as well as interest, compassion, and concern. The demands of servant leadership, no matter how difficult, are not met with reluctance or resistance. This is in direct contrast with demands for self-sacrifice imposed by obligation or position of power. Stephen did not flinch at the demand that cost him his life. Philip did not drag his feet or plead exemption when the Lord told him to start out on a fifty mile hike down a lonely desert road.

Servant leaders are willing to pay the price of preparation. They are not soft or easy on themselves or their students. They set high, uncompromising standards without flaunting authority. Stephen's defense before the

Sanhedrin was not an informal, extemporaneous speech, delivered "off the cuff" or "the top of his head." It was a carefully condensed history of God's people, climaxing in a stinging rebuke for their rejection and murder of the Righteous One.

Philip's opening of the scripture to the Ethiopian was not accomplished simply by reading aloud what the man had already read for himself. Philip must have studied to understand clearly enough to explain the meaning to another, and then to lead the conversation through steps of enlightenment, decision, and action.

Wisdom comes from God, and God chooses to bestow this gift to those who engage in the disciplines of study and observation, learning through life experiences, and recording in one's memory many of the lessons patiently learned.

Servant Leaders Are Willing to Stand

All leaders face criticism and rejection. The rejection is more often of an idea than of the leader as a person. But even that is not easy to take, since our ideas are part of ourselves. Servant leaders patiently and quietly continue on a steady course.

Servant leaders realize they have a place in this world and are at home in it. They do not need to rationalize or explain their position. They do not have to attribute their leadership assignment to "those higher up." Some leaders find it important to establish their credentials in order to prove their critics wrong. Others are quickly discouraged by criticism, embittered by opposition, and give in to defeat.

How different the defense of Stephen when he was criticized, falsely accused, unjustly sentenced, and finally stoned to death. His face was not flushed with anger, but the inner glow of an angelic spirit. His last words were not vengeful threats, but tranquil release and forgiveness.

Servant Leaders Are Guided by the Heart

Servant leaders see assignments in proportion to the opportunity to serve. Joy in serving is never measured in recognition, titles, degrees, or certificates. Leaders are tempted to use many and varied standards of measurement in deciding whether to accept or decline a particular assignment. Some frequently used include the following:

"How does it fit with my skills and interests?"

"Is the pay adequate (or in line with present scales)?"

"Will this assignment enhance my reputation as a leader?"

"What additional benefits, such as additional training or security for the future, are included?"

"Are the equipment, supplies, and other resources provided the best available?"

"Is the environment (classroom, office) comfortable and convenient?"

"Will I have team members with whom I can work cooperatively, and enough assistance to get the job done?"

Any or all of these may be appropriate measures to a certain extent in leadership decisions. But the only measure that is one-hundred percent valid for the servant leader must be, "Where is the greatest opportunity for service?" For the servant leader, the heart guides the actions and the decisions.

When Stephen and Philip accepted the assignment to assist five others to administer charity to the needy of the community, none of the earlier questions could have prompted their decision to say yes. Only hearts filled to overflowing with the love of Christ and eyes that perceived the need with the compassion of Christ would have been challenged by this simple invitation to join the servant corps.

Philip is referred to as the "evangelist." But the term in the first-century church was not reserved for a preacher of great renown who moved great crowds of people with powerful sermons. Evangelists in Philip's day as today were those who faithfully proclaimed the gospel as they spoke and wrote about Jesus, bringing his message to others.

It is recorded of both Stephen and Philip that they did "great wonders and miraculous signs among the people." But in the context of the other things they did and said, it is impossible to conclude that the miracles and great wonders were performed to bring acclaim to themselves. We can only believe that two men so filled with the Spirit performed extraordinary acts because they were moved by the needs of persons around them, and saw through these acts widening opportunities to serve.

Servant Leaders Are Leaders

A servant leader may not be *the* leader but is a special kind of leader—and one who makes a difference. Christ did not reject the idea of greatness. He specifically claimed greatness for his kingdom and its members— those who belong to Christ. Leaders are called to greatness rather than mediocrity or triviality. The paradox is in the way to greatness Jesus pointed out to his disciples: "You know that the rulers of the Gentiles lord it over them, and their high officials exercise authority over them. Not so with you. Instead, whoever wants to become great among you must be your servant, and whoever wants to be first must be your slave—just as the Son of Man did not come to be served, but to serve, and to give his life as a ransom for many" (Matt. 20:25-28).

This astonishing idea acted out by the early Christian leaders like Stephen and Philip turned the world upside down. The kind of leadership that makes a difference is greatness expressed by the voluntary acceptance of the servant status. "The word of God spread. The number of disciples in Jerusalem increased rapidly, and a large number of priests became obedient to the faith" (Acts

187

6:7). "Those who had been scattered [because of perse-cution of Christians in Jerusalem] preached the word wherever they went. Philip went down to a city in Samaria and proclaimed the Christ there. When the crowds heard Philip and saw the miraculous signs he did, they all paid close attention to what he said. With shrieks, evil spirits came out of many, and many paralytics and cripples were healed. So there was great joy in that city" (Acts 8:4-8).

A servant leader should work to achieve the highest level of competence possible—to develop increasing cap-abilities—and expand horizons into a future filled with challenge and hope. But the competence and capabilities will be achieved primarily for others rather than the leader's own satisfaction. The mark of greatness for any Christian is not personal reward but continued expansion of opportunities to serve.

"The ultimate test of servanthood is that those who are being served, by the way they are served ultimately become disposed themselves to be servants."* Certainly Stephen and Philip passed this ultimate test of servant-hood. Christians in every generation since Stephen have been inspired and challenged by his exceptional defense of the gospel of Jesus Christ and by his fearless and forgiving spirit.

Scripture tells us that after the Ethiopian's conversion and baptism he continued on his journey with great joy! Bible story writers have often added that he went with joy and excitement to tell all he met in his country about Jesus, his Savior.

Yes, servant leaders lead and their serving makes a difference!

Servant Leaders Are Messengers

These are people who do not forget the message or neglect their assignment as messengers. It is all too easy to get so caught up in the message that delivering the message is postponed. Some leaders get so intent on studying the Bible that biblical knowledge and understanding become a self-serving goal.

On the other hand, some focus all their attention on developing innovative, effective methods for delivering the message until enthusiastic, qualified messengers discover they have no message to deliver. In Stephen's defense before the Sanhedrin and in Philip's encounter with the Ethiopian official, we experience a vital, compelling message from a committed and capable servant leader.

Notes

*Robert K. Greenleaf, *Teacher as Servant* (Paulist Press, 1979), 29.

Chapter 12
Barnabas: Supportive Leadership

A. Barnabas

by Kenneth F. Hall

Paul and Barnabas had been in the town of Lystra for several days now. They had arrived here after a journey with many ups and downs. In fact they had just fled here from Iconium to escape a threatened stoning. Preaching the gospel wasn't easy with all the hardships of the journey, the opposition of unbelievers, the misunderstanding of people with only pagan experience behind them. What happened now may have been like this:

Barnabas looked at his younger friend striding alongside him and noted the eager glint that came into Paul's eyes as he saw a small group of people standing visiting with each other in the shady corner of the square they were now approaching.

"I think they heard we were coming back today," Paul said. "They want to hear more."

"And you will tell them in no uncertain terms," agreed Barnabas as he gave his friend a gentle tap on the shoulder. He had watched Paul grow in his speaking skills and in his confidence along the hard road of their travels. Seeing this happen had been good, Barnabas thought. Of course, the church at Antioch might be a bit surprised to see exactly what had happened. When they were first commissioned to go out to carry the news of Jesus Christ to this part of the world, people had assumed that Barnabas would be the leader. After all, Barnabas was the older, the more experienced preacher, a man regarded as equal with the original apostles themselves. Barnabas was the wise one, the diplomat, the leader who had come from Jerusalem itself to help in the pioneering church efforts in Asia Minor. But along the way Barnabas had come to realize more and more what a tremendous preacher, teacher, and leader this Paul was. Barnabas had patiently coached him, supported him, and encouraged him in the hard times—and now Paul was taking the lead. Paul made the big moves. It was he who preached to the largest crowds.

Barnabas Stands By

Barnabas spoke again as they drew near the little group in the square. "I'll be standing here while you speak. I'll keep an eye on things. I'll probably find someone with some questions that I can deal with, and when you need someone to say Amen, I'll be ready." Paul smiled at his friend and waded into the crowd. They were curious about what he would have today. After they had all exchanged greetings for awhile, Paul launched into his talk, speaking fluently in the common Greek of the day, a language the Lystrans could well understand and use even through they had their own language in this region.

Even as Paul spoke, Barnabas kept a sharp eye on the crowd. He noticed at one side a man sitting with his back propped against a shop wall.

Barnabas noted the eagerness in the man's eyes, the way he leaned just a bit forward in spite of the handicap that obviously kept him sitting on the hard, cold stones of the town square. Here was someone who was searching for more than a chance to walk. Here was a man in whom faith was being born, who through Paul's introduction was coming to the point where he would invite Jesus Christ into his life.

192

Barnabas was touched by compassion. Out of the side of his vision he could also see Paul watching the man with that same look of concern. In fact Paul paused in his words to the people and turned to the sitting man. He breathed a prayer for the healing of the man—and then he called out: "Stand up straight on your feet!"

The crippled man leaped up. He took some quick short steps, the first in his life. He walked rapidly around the square, an unbelieving look, of joy on his face, and with every other step he took he turned to look once more at the man who had given him this healing command.

Barnabas stood watching the scene. His own prayer had joined Paul's, and now he also shared in the rejoicing over the miracle that had happened to this seeking man with such a great need. Barnabas noted that the people were talking excitedly with each other. They were using their own language now, and so he couldn't be sure exactly what they were saying. But they seemed to be looking first at Paul and then at himself with awe and perhaps fear. They were standing back from Paul now. One man pointed toward the sky. A woman came and bowed at Barnabas' feet. In a moment Barnabas thought he saw someone point at Paul and cry, "Hermes!" And then another came to Barnabas excitedly and said, "Zeus."

It was only a moment before the meaning came through to Barnabas. He found his way through the engulfing throng to talk developments over with Paul. "Do you know what is going on here?"

"I'm afraid we are in the middle of a case of mistaken identity. They must think we are some kind of gods."

"You are right. I thought I heard one of them calling you *Hermes,*" said Barnabas. "That fits, since they could clearly tell that here you have been the messenger, the preacher."

"And you, my friend," added Paul, "have been called *Zeus.* It must be that distinguished gray hair and obvious wisdom about you that makes them think of you as the chief god of their whole pantheon."

Mistaken Identity

Now the man who had been healed came up and began talking with them, expressing his joy. He also passed along the word about just what had been happening. "My friends here have been shouting, 'The gods have come down to us in the likeness of men.' They are getting ready to worship you. Some have gone for garlands to put on your heads. Some are preparing oxen for sacrifice. Oh, you are indeed great men. How glad I am that you have come to our city and that you have seen fit to heal me."

Both Paul and Barnabas were nonplussed. Embarrassed, Barnabas searched for the words to help the man to understand that it was the power of Christ and the love and care of the Christian community that had been involved in the healing. At the same time, something must be done to stop the mistaken, pagan worship that was unfolding. Already Paul was rushing out into the middle of the square, tearing his cloak and shouting to the people. He grabbed one man who was trying to put a wreath on his head and violently shook his head.

"People of Lystra! Why are you doing this? We are human just like you. We simply come to urge you to turn from empty and foolish things to the true God who made the heaven, the earth, and the sea and all that is in them."

The people were at least stopping now to listen. The priest out at the temple of Zeus probably was still gathering up his material for a sacrifice at the city gate. But here the people had stopped long enough to listen while Paul continued to speak.

"In past generations the Lord God allowed all nations to walk in their own ways. Yet he did not leave himself without witness, for he did good and gave you from heaven rains and fruitful seasons, satisfying your hearts with food and gladness."

By now, however, the people were so swept away by their adulation of these visitors that they could not really hear the words. They still came pressing their gifts and their praise on Paul and Barnabas.

To quiet the uneasy situation, the pair slipped away from the crowd and returned to the rooms provided for them by friends of their mission. There they could rest and think over their situation.

"This is far different from what we had back there in Iconium, isn't it?" Barnabas said. "We had to run for our lives from there. They didn't think we were gods. Far from it."

"And we shall have to run for our lives again," added Paul. "Maybe even from this place. The people's background is so pagan that they can hardly begin to understand what we are all about."

Barnabas went back in his mind over several events that had led him to this spot. Always he seemed to be dealing with misunderstandings as he tried to help people reach new insights. His leadership had been there. He had been recognized and appreciated. People thought he was a genuine follower of Christ, a totally admirable person. The church had come close at times to worshiping him in its own way. There was always so much misunderstanding.

Son of Encouragement

For instance, there was the time that a young and fiery Paul had suddenly appeared at Jerusalem. The church there was not about to accept this persecutor of the Christians into its fellowship even though they had heard his claims of a radical conversion to Christ on the Damascus road. But Barnabas saw the potential in him and believed his testimony. He took Paul to the church and recommended him to them. He set the example by welcoming Paul to his own house and being his friend. Paul preached to the people in Jerusalem and won his way with them. No wonder, Barnabas remembered, that he had come to be known among the Jerusalem Christians as Barnabas—son of Encouragement—more than by his actual given name of Joseph.

Then Barnabas remembered how the home church at Jerusalem had sent him off to Antioch in Syria to work with the young and growing group of Christians there. It was good to have this link through him between the older church at Jerusalem and the exciting new work in Antioch, particularly since other natives of Cyprus were involved there, too. As the work grew, Barnabas had a clear enough picture of his own skills and limitations to recognize when he needed help. He remembered Paul now laboring in his home territory around Tarsus, and he had gone up there to recruit him for leadership in Antioch.

This had brought Paul to the forefront in the leadership of the church. He accompanied Barnabas back to Jerusalem when they took a famine relief offering to the home church.

Later Barnabas could remember with a warm glow when the church at Antioch had decided to send Paul and him out on a mission to support and establish new congregations. Barnabas' young nephew John Mark would go with them. Barnabas would informally head the mission. That would change as they went along. Paul with his great skills and strength of personality would become more of the leader of the expedition. But that was all right with Barnabas. He was glad to see Paul gain in influence and increasingly fill an important niche in the church.

Oh, it had hurt when they had come to a disagreement over John Mark. Not everyone had the ability to see the potential in people the way Barnabas did even in the midst of discouraging times and disappointments. But they were making their way, and one day John Mark would prove his worth in the church. Even now young John was working with Peter, serving as his secretary and becoming an increasingly valuable assistant.

As Barnabas reflected now he thought also of the growing rift in the church between those who wished to keep all the requirements of the Jewish law in the church's practice and those who wanted the greater freedom to attract Greeks and to focus more completely on Christ. Barnabas considered himself something of a diplomat in that situation even when he had to oppose Paul and others when it came to sorting out the distinctions in dispute.

Meantime here in Lystra he and Paul would continue to spread the gospel. Wherever they could find anyone to listen they would preach and teach. That young man who was healed today would help to supply a further base for their work, Barnabas hoped. But before long, Barnabas knew in his heart, the enemies of the church would catch up with them here. Their lives would be threatened, and they would move on to a new challenge.

Eventually, he knew, too, that he and Paul would need to part. Perhaps he would return to his beloved native land of Cyprus, and there he would spend the rest of his years quietly establishing the kingdom of God on ever firmer ground.

B: Supportive Leadership

by Jim B. Luttrell

Barnabas: Who Was He?

The name *Barnabas* means "son of encouragement" or "son of comfort." Barnabas was identified as an apostle of the secondary group. That is, he was not one of the original twelve. The term apostle seems to carry with it a specific commission or responsibility for leadership. He was originally named Joseph. We are told that he most likely received the name Barnabas because of his preaching style.

Barnabas belonged to the company of the first converts in Jerusalem who were won by the preaching of the apostles or perhaps even by Jesus. He was a leader of the Antioch church, and the one, along with Paul, who carried relief funds from Antioch to famine-stricken Jerusalem (Acts 11:30). He was a companion of Paul on the mission to Cyprus and Pisidia. Referred to as the "working apostle" by Paul, Barnabas was clearly seen as a bridge-builder between the Jewish and Greek elements in the church.

The Character of Barnabas

When Barnabas arrived at Antioch we find this statement about him in Acts 11:23, 24: "When he arrived and saw how God blessed the people, he was glad and urged them all to be faithful and true to the Lord with all their hearts. Barnabas was a good man, full of the Holy Spirit and faith, and many people were brought to the Lord" (TEV).

Barnabas was sent by the Christian leaders in Jerusalem to Antioch where a phenomenon of the church was taking place. There was widespread prejudice against the Gentiles, and the gospel was being preached openly to them for the first time. The fact that the Jews sent Barnabas indicates that they saw some extraordinary qualities of leadership in him.

Barnabas was referred to as "good." We know that good refers to the character or nature of a person, not the absence of humanity or of faults. One can have high moral standards, be law-abiding, and yet be a person who is selfish, cold, uncaring, or unloving. It seems very obvious both from his treatment of others and his high recommendations from others that this was not the case with Barnabas.

Other characteristics of Barnabas were his warm spirit, gentle nature, the desire and ability to nurture (pastor) people. He did not seem to have any strong ego need for recognition or position or even for a sense of authority.

Perhaps it could even be said that Barnabas served as a mentor to Paul and John Mark. A mentor is defined as a teacher, coach, or adviser. But in my experience a mentor is more than that. A mentor is one who personally invests time and faith in the leadership abilities as well as the life of another. A mentor would even take risks in the development of the leadership of another. Barnabas stood firm on his convictions, but he did not abandon John Mark because he made some bad choices or because he was being criticized by others. Barnabas was steadfast in his relationships.

Mark defected at Cyprus; consequently, Paul dropped him from the team. But Barnabas was devoted to Mark and took him on a separate mission to Cyprus. Furthermore, Barnabas put people above things. He sold property to help the church minister to the poor and needy. He was apparently a man of means, but he never flaunted that or used it to buy position or influence. In this way, Barnabas not only demonstrated unselfishness but he also earned a right, based on Christian principles, to be the leader he had already become.

Barnabas recognized leadership potential. When there

was disagreement between himself and Paul and between Paul and John Mark, he could have easily discredited or undermined Paul or even written him off as a potential leader. But he saw beyond the immediate situation and invested himself in helping a potential leader not only to survive but also to be able to blossom forth as a great leader. Apparently Barnabas knew how to stand firm in his convictions with a definite sense of direction, and yet he did not run over others in the process of being a leader. He knew who he was, where he had come from, and where he was going. He was secure in his leadership role.

Barnabas was obviously a team person. Deliberations and negotiations were undoubtedly a part of the process at Antioch before the missionaries were commissioned. Team ministry or leadership is defined as two or more persons working together in a coordinated effort toward a defined purpose or objective. Webster defines teamwork as "joint action by a group of people, in which individual interests are subordinated to group unity and efficiency." Barnabas obviously employed this concept in his relationships and particularly in his approach to encouraging and supporting others in their ministry efforts.

Leadership Distinctives

Although Luke clearly identifies Barnabas as the leader of the church at Antioch and Acts shows that Barnabas was certainly accepted as a leader in the Diaspora, nevertheless modern scholars have given preeminence to Paul's teachings and life. It was Barnabas who introduced and favorably recommended Paul, the new convert, to the disciples in Jerusalem. This indicates that Barnabas' leadership was well accepted and his opinions valued.

Although in the beginning Luke and Acts refer to "Barnabas and Paul," on the island of Cyprus Paul took over the leadership of the ministry and thereafter they were known as "Paul and Company." However, in Lystra the natives gave Barnabas the name of "Zeus" and Paul was only called "Hermes," the spokesman. "The men of Lystra must have recognized a comparative dignity in Barnabas." (*Interpreter's Dictionary of the Bible*, I, 356).

Although Paul assumed leadership in Lystra it seems that Paul's leadership was temporarily suspended after he was stoned. Barnabas does not appear to have been stoned. When Barnabas was commissioned to go out the church could have assumed that he would be the leader since he was the oldest and an experienced preacher and teacher. In addition, he was the one who was from Jerusalem and who was evidently held in equal regard with the original apostles. Yet, Barnabas, recognizing the potential and the leadership qualities of Paul, encouraged Paul, supported and advised him, until, finally it seems that Paul's leadership became preeminent.

Why and How Do Persons Become Leaders?

Sometimes leaders are appointed by a higher authority or by a person or persons who have a higher position. For instance, the political party in power often chooses persons for certain offices. Sometimes leaders are recognized because of a title they have. Prince Charles would be this kind of example. Then sometimes people have no particular title or position, but because of personality and certain leadership qualities, they emerge as leaders or "earn" the function of leadership. Leaders in the church often fit into this category. Many who are elected or appointed to a "position" soon realize that position without ability or "right of leadership" is empty. Unless some leadership skill can be quickly demonstrated, this type of person is soon disregarded as a leader.

Then there are those who exhibit certain gifts or abilities and thereby become leaders. The latter often become leaders of distinction based upon an outstanding singular gift. John F. Kennedy, for instance, was recognized for his vigor, his youthful aspirations, and his unique ability to communicate in fresh, exciting ways.

Sam Rayburn, the long-term Speaker of the House of Representatives, was recognized as a powerful personality and one who had "influence" among his colleagues. Washington church leader Dr. Sam Hines is one who is honored in leadership by his diplomatic personality and his atypical ability to communicate, in addition to being held in high regard for his Christian character.

Some people desire positions of leadership; others have bestowed upon them the mantle of leadership; still others "inherit" the qualities that seem to thrust them into leadership positions. Those who desire it usually work hard to acquire skills and abilities that will qualify them for leadership positions. Still others may work at it for a lifetime and seem just not to be in the right place at the right time. All in all, leadership seems to be a combination of acquired and learned skills, inherited traits, and some chance.

Implications for Leadership in the Church

Perhaps the church has been done a disservice through the model of business and industry in positional style leadership. Often more credence is given to the office—president, chairperson of the board, director, vice-president—than to the tasks to be accomplished and the quality of persons needed for the fulfillment of those tasks.

I particularly like designations that are a job description rather than an ecclesiastical title. A designation such as "minister of pastoral care" or "minister of outreach and discipleship" describes in brief the area of responsibility of a person and points to the function of ministry as opposed to titles like "assistant minister" or "senior minister," which refer to positions more than to the ministry function. In addition, the latter title sounds as if it underlines an administrative responsibility rather than a relational one, which I believe ministry implies.

Many leaders of our time would base their willingness to take a certain job upon the degree of authority given them by the job or upon the title or even upon the power they have to administer a program according to their own desires. Leadership is better served if one attempts to match needs with skills and gifts rather than a degree of authority.

Sometimes "team" leadership is looked upon as lacking in direction or authority. Not so! Depending upon the function or task and whose ability matches the task, leadership emerges on a cooperative rather than a competitive basis. The question is not, "Who's in charge?" but, "What needs to be done and whose gifts best match the need?" In this role, one leader takes the initiative and another lends supportive leadership and encourages the process in a positive and caring way. What's important is the mission to be accomplished and not who gets the credit for a job well done. Team leadership is healthy because it recognizes the worth of another person on an equal basis and because it encourages leaders to develop and grow by mutual supportiveness and confidence in areas where they may not have been encouraged to take a leadership role before. All members of a team are seen as being equally important—just different in function.

Persons who are secure in who they are and who like who they are make effective leaders. This underscores the need in the local church for discipling of new Christians. Immaturity and insecurity account for many problems and crises in leadership in the church. Maturing Christians can confront caringly and openly and can be constructive in their advice or suggestions rather than acting in threatening or negative ways toward their co-workers. Unconditional love demonstrates itself in positive and nonthreatening ways.

Barnabas demonstrated the ability of being able, first, to recognize the ability in another and then to encourage and support that person to the point of perhaps even being replaced by the newfound leader. This is a rare quality of leadership but a very desirable and healthy one!

Barnabas: A Model of Christian Leadership

Barnabas seemed to be a confident person yet not arrogant or conceited. In his actions he was not hesitant or unsure or faltering. On the contrary he seemed to have a plan, to be decisive and to be able and willing to take risks. He did not gain the notoriety of others in the New Testament, even of those he sought to encourage and disciple such as Paul. He was not noted as a great preacher and he was not a founder of any church. Clearly, however, the people of the Jerusalem church as well as his newfound associates in Antioch saw him as a leader who had a firm foundation of faith, who was trustworthy and reliable, who was diplomatic in relationships, and whom other leaders looked to for the qualities needed for the task to be done.

Indeed, his generous spirit, his loyalty to his friends and associates, his willingness to promote someone else instead of himself, his willingness to serve out of love, not control, his deep sense of caring, his unconditional love, and his redemptive attitude toward others are all qualities of Christlikeness that Barnabas attained and that all of us as leaders should strive for!

A Barnabas Style of Leadership Means

Supportive Leadership
A Servant Attitude
A Redemptive Spirit
A Sensitivity to the Qualities in Others
Unconditional Love
Caring
A Forgiving Nature
Being Thoroughly Unselfish
Positive Thinking
An Encourager
A Helpful Nature
One Who Puts People Above Things

Chapter 13
Paul: Gifts and Leadership

A. Paul

by Fredrick H. Shively

"For me to live is Christ." This statement, simple yet profound, epitomizes the deep personal commitment that characterizes the life of the man from Tarsus known as Paul, apostle to the Gentiles. As one reads Doctor Luke's account of Paul's adventures or the apostle's own firsthand version of his life in his letters, one readily sees the transparency of this man. He stands open to all who look at him; his humanness, foibles, temper, sarcasm, loves, brilliance, and intensity are all in plain view—and all of it is there to point through him to the one who captured his heart, Jesus of Nazareth, known to Paul as Jesus Christ, the Son of God.

Although Paul probably never met Jesus in the flesh, he was captivated by him. "In Christ" became the central expression throughout his writings. We gain no clear understanding of Paul's thought apart from his passionate references to the Christ. "I can do all things through him [Christ] who strengthens me," he wrote. The identification was so strong that he also said, "Be imitators of me, as I am of the Christ."

It is not that the apostle would ever elevate himself to the same level as "the Christ." His goal was to become so transparent that the Christ-spirit became visible through him and the Christ-life relevant and practical.

How did such a deep commitment come to be experienced by one known as Saul, a Pharisee, zealous persecutor of Christians, and what were the results of the transformation brought about by his encounter with the Christ?

Tarsus to Jerusalem

Saul was born a few years after the birth of Jesus. During that time Augustine, the Roman emperor, maintained the lenient treatment of the Jews that Julius Caesar had begun. The province of Cilicia was at peace under Roman control. The Jews there were unmolested; among them, Saul's father even enjoyed Roman citizenship.

Not all of the citizens of Tarsus held Roman citizenship, although Antony had granted the city the status of *urbs libera,* a free city. Perhaps Saul's grandfather had earned the status of citizen for services rendered in civil wars. Saul had inherited this privilege.

Tarsus was prosperous, cosmopolitan, located on a major East-West trade route. Opportunities for education were good. The people of Tarsus, caught up in recent Roman history and influenced by both Roman and Greek philosophy, were eager to pursue culture, higher learning—the liberal arts, the whole "encyclopedia" of knowledge.

The contrast to the Galilean village of Nazareth is striking. Of that little town, people frequently asked, "Can any good come out of Nazareth?" Yet the effect of one from Nazareth over the man from Tarsus was to be dramatic.

Roman law and Greek philosophy were not the only influences in Saul's early life. As a member of a dedicated Jewish family, he was given the heritage of his Jewish ancestors. The threefold Talmudic tradition, "circumcize him, teach him the law, and teach him a trade," surely was not wasted on Saul.

Rabbi Judah had said. "If you do not teach your son a

trade, you teach him to be a thief." Paul's own mentor, Rabban Gamaliel, had added, "To what would you compare the one who has a trade in his hand? He is like a vineyard that is fenced." And what better training for Saul than to learn to weave home-grown goat hair, known as cilicium, into water-resistant tent material? This trade would be in great demand throughout Saul's life.

Saul became an avid student of Jewish law. Born into a family of Pharisees, of the tribe of Benjamin, he gained a great respect for all of the law, both written and oral. For him the Scripture consisted of three parts—the Torah, the Prophets, and the Writings. He marveled at how "Abraham trusted God, and it was reckoned to him as righteousness." He read in the prophet Habakkuk, "The righteous shall live by his faith."

The Pharisees were the enthusiasts of Judaism. Eager to make proselytes, they held great influence over the people. Rallying around the law became the center of their unity. They gave themselves studiously to its interpretation. They delighted in multiplying the requirements of the truly dedicated. They demanded liberality in almsgiving, frequent fasting, long public prayers, keeping of the smallest details of the law. They were ostentatious in their practice; others marveled at their religiosity. Saul later testified that under the law he was flawless. As Judaism spread and endured, the Pharisees were its hope. Though they couldn't defend the city of Jerusalem, they could with great skill and persuasion defend the Law.

Paul's family were his first teachers, and then they made it possible for him to sit at the feet of the greatest expositor of the Law at that time, the teacher Gamaliel. The son of Simeon and grandson of the great Rabbi Hillel, Gamaliel was the only rabbi granted the honorific title of "Rabban—our Master, our Great one." He was also an honored member of the Sanhedrin; later he demonstrated great charity in response to Peter and other disciples when they were called before the Sanhedrin.

So, Saul's education—both the liberal arts and a thorough grounding in religious instruction—prepared him for life as a Jewish Pharisee in a Greco-Roman world. His education was not complete, however. He was yet to experience the spiritual dimension that would prepare him for his greatest task. He could not have predicted the change that awaited him. Education as a Pharisee provided layers to buffer him from a hostile world; his surprise encounter with one he considered an enemy was to tear those layers away.

Jerusalem to Damascus

Avid in everything he did, Saul set out to prove himself worthy of recognition as a dedicated Pharisee; he joined in the task of persecuting a small group of Jews known as "The Way," who claimed to have known the Messiah. Paul was determined to force these heretics to renounce their newfound faith and again to embrace Jewish tradition.

In this pursuit he met Stephen. Recently appointed to ·care for widows, Stephen was greatly respected within this new community of messianic believers. He was called to give an account of his teaching before the Jewish high court of seventy, the Sanhedrin. The solemn meeting took place on the temple mount, partly within the court.

Stephen was accused of blasphemy, a crime punishable by death. He answered the questions of his accusers clearly and without hesitation. He recited the history of the Jews, demonstrating his own thorough Jewishness. The leaders listened with interest and even pride as he made his way from Abraham to Moses to David, employing a method that young Saul himself would develop in years to come.

But at the end of his message, Stephen looked these men in the eye and cried, "You stiff-necked people always resist the Holy Spirit. Your fathers killed the prophets, and you have killed the Righteous One." As they ground their teeth in rage, he looked up and said, "I see the Son of Man standing at the right hand of God."

It was too much for the council. Like a mob, they dragged him into the streets of Jerusalem, through the gates to a point where the city overlooks the adjacent valley. Without pausing, they savagely hurled stones until he was dead.

Anyone watching the event that day from any vantage point northeast of the city would have seen the crowd tossing their outer garments at the feet of a young man who stood by, approving. But they could not have heard the words that Saul heard that day, words that he would never be able to forget, a prayer from the dying Stephen: "Lord, do not hold this sin against them." Saul did not realize that those were essentially the same words spoken by another dying man, Jesus, as he prayed from the cross: "Father, forgive them; for they know not what they do." Through this prayer, though unaware, Saul met the Christ. He was never able to forget the moment.

After Stephen's death, Saul persisted in his practice of persecuting believers in the Christ. He broke into their meetings, entered their homes, and threw many of them into prison. His aggressiveness made his name one to be feared. Because of this persecution, the disciples fled Jerusalem. The result was that believers were springing up everywhere in many new locations.

In Damascas the new groups had grown strong, and Saul determined to go there. As Saul and his companions passed the Sea of Tiberias, they entered the area known as Galilee, where Jesus grew up. Did Saul know it was the home of the man whose followers he pursued with such vehemence? The road turned northeast within sight of snow-capped Mount Hermon, a view that must have refreshed Saul as he made his way through the barren desert, stony hills and dry plains, the sun burning hot overhead.

When Damascus finally came into view, Saul must have welcomed the sight. The oldest continuously inhabited city in the world, Damascus was filled with vegetation, gardens, and fruit trees along its river banks. It was the end of a long journey for the driven persecutor of the Messiah's followers.

But it was to be the beginning of an even longer journey. Just outside the city, as Saul eagerly approached his destination at noon, a great light suddenly knocked him to his knees. The encounter that followed is difficult to explain. Its accounts vary. Whatever his companions experienced, Saul met one he immediately recognized to be the Christ. Prostrate, he heard the words, "Saul, why are you persecuting me?" The apostle later wrote of this experience, "Have I not seen Jesus our Lord?" It was to be his call, as authentic as that of any other apostle of Jesus Christ. Although the details of this dramatic event cannot be described exactly, it is clear that Saul, later to be known as Paul, was never after that the same.

A vastly different, humble Saul was led into Damascus, where a believer named Ananias was ready to take care of him. Protection was necessary because the Christian believers were still afraid of him, and his former Jewish friends on hearing of his experience were now angry enough to kill him. A new life had begun for Saul, to be filled with peril, excitement, and spiritual growth.

Damascus to Arabia

Escaping from Damascus over the city wall in a basket, Saul traveled into Arabia for a period of spiritual exile. During the next years he learned about life in the Spirit.

Saul began by entering into a time of reflection, on his own learning, on the death of Stephen, and especially his conversion encounter with the Christ. He undoubtedly reread the Scriptures, now with a different vision of their meaning. He felt called to be an apostle—a missionary—of this gospel to the greater Gentile world.

Later he adamantly declared that his call came not from any human person but only through a revelation of Jesus Christ. This period of reflection and learning lasted fourteen or seventeen years before he was ready to become part of the fellowship of believers in Jerusalem and later, Antioch.

Antioch to Asia to Europe

Saul knew his own heart. Daily he was experiencing growth in his relationship with the one he would later describe in intimate terms. Daily he gained new insights about himself, insights that he would freely share in preaching and writing. Saul was still in need of a human mediator, however, someone to speak in his behalf who could urge other believers to accept him. Saul could not have become a leader within the early Christian community if it had never granted him the privilege. Leadership cannot be seized; it must be granted. He found a mediator in Barnabas. Called by his fellows "the Son of Consolation," Barnabas helped remove all suspicion held toward Saul by the community of believers.

These two friends, Barnabas and Saul, became part of the Church in Antioch. They spent a happy year there, studying, teaching and preaching, receiving visiting believers, watching the congregation grow, and planning how to reach the world with the gospel. The citizens of Antioch called them *Christians,* a new term that, no matter how it was first given, came to have special meaning to the believers.

The church in Antioch became the great launching pad for the missionary movement. When the time came to consecrate missionaries for service, they selected their finest, Barnabas and Saul. It is not coincidental that their first assignment was on the island of Cypress; Barnabas was a land owner there. As they left Antioch, he was clearly the leader.

On this little island, with its mountain summits in view

from the mainland, a change took place in the evangelistic company, perhaps little noted at the time. As Barnabas and Saul appeared before the proconsul, a magician named Elymas attempted to intervene. Saul boldly confronted him, amazing the proconsul and leading him to believe in their message. Saul then became known by the Roman name Paul and as they left the island, he had become the obvious leader of the group. He was to exercise this leadership for the rest of his ministry, becoming the premier "apostle to the Gentiles." His ministry with Barnabas and Mark, later Silas, Luke, Timothy, Titus, Epaphroditus, and many others, took him through Asia, into Europe, and eventually to Rome itself. Everywhere they went believers were established, Jews and Gentiles alike.

Return to Jerusalem

Paul's ministry to the Gentile world was not to go unchallenged, however. The challenge came in a form that threatened to divide the fellowship of believers into two irreconcilable camps. The leaders of the church in Jerusalem had become greatly concerned about the large number of Gentile converts. Should they not first subject themselves to Jewish tradition in order to become *bona fide* believers? Paul and Barnabas hurried anxiously to Jerusalem for the confrontation. No doubt the church in Antioch prayed for their success.

The problem these leaders faced at that Jerusalem Conference was both religious and social. Much of Jewish tradition enforced isolation on the Jews. They saw themselves to have been particularly chosen and blessed by God. They allowed converts, but those proselytes had to undergo a rigorous initiation to their new faith, which included practices such as circumcision, dietary laws, and moral and social codes. This particularism had been naturally inherited by Jewish Christians who saw themselves simply as true Jews.

Paul did not have to rehearse how he would address the leaders in Jerusalem; he was unafraid to be open and confrontive. His report of this meeting to the churches of Galatia is straightforward.

When Paul and Barnabas arrived in Jerusalem, their first encounter was with Peter. The fisherman from Galilee was still in the middle of a conversion to a universal faith. The vision in Joppa and conversion of the Roman centurion Cornelius had done much to open his eyes, but he was easily influenced by those of stronger persuasion, particularly James, Jesus' brother, the leader of the church in Jerusalem.

Meeting with Peter, Paul and Barnabas enlisted his support. In Antioch Peter had eaten with Gentile believers, and Paul reminded him of this in strong language. He directed forceful words toward the waffling Peter: "If you, though a Jew, live like a Gentile and not like a Jew, how can you compel the Gentiles to live like Jews?" But it was the meeting with James that was pivotal. James, too, finally endorsed the work of Paul and Barnabas, and with a few conditions sent them back to Antioch with the Jerusalem church's blessing. A potential tragedy for the church was thus averted.

Jerusalem to Rome

The strategy of Paul and his fellow workers was to go into a major city—Ephesus, Philippi, Corinth, Athens—first to the local synagogue (if there was one), and to proclaim the crucifixion-resurrection and messiahship of Jesus. After the establishment of some Jewish converts, the apostles and their new converts would leave the synagogue and begin meeting in a more general place—a hall, a house, a river bank—and the church would be established in that city.

In most places the apostles were met with great opposition, usually from infuriated Jews. Paul was beaten and left for dead (Lystra), imprisoned (Philippi, Ephesus), and laughed at (Athens). Still they went on, persisting, enduring whatever persecution came and preaching without fear for their lives. Their perseverance resulted in the establishment of church after church. Patiently, lovingly, openly Paul corresponded with these churches to teach and strengthen them. Through his pen he poured out his heart without regard for the effect upon himself. He wept, used sarcasm, lavished affection, confronted problems, and gave encouragement and instruction. He confessed his humanness, asked for forgiveness, and loved deeply.

Eventually Paul felt compelled to return to Jerusalem. His friends warned him against such a trip, knowing his life was in jeopardy. But Paul insisted. The parallels to Jesus' earlier journey to Jerusalem are striking. Both knew that they faced certain danger in Jerusalem, but both knew that Paul must make the journey. As he departed, Paul and the Ephesian leaders wept together in an emotional farewell.

The fears of Paul's friends were realized. Jews of the Dispersion visiting Jerusalem recognized him as the troublemaker in their home city. After a near riot Paul was arrested for his own safe-keeping and imprisoned in Caesarea. After two years, because he appealed to Caesar as a Roman citizen, he was placed aboard a ship enroute from Alexandria to Rome. His long-sought dream of preaching in Rome was finally to be realized, though it had not come as he had expected.

The journey to Rome was arduous and life-threatening. A storm destroyed the ship and they were stranded on the island of Malta. Through a miraculous series of events the prisoner became the one who epitomized hope for the frightened crew.

As they disembarked in Puteoli, Paul was met by Christians from Rome, and they traveled joyfully along the Appian Way into the greatest city of their world. Although he was technically under house arrest, the apostle to the Gentiles continued to preach and teach and write openly for at least two years. Paul expounded on the Scriptures and taught freely about the kingdom of God and the lordship of Jesus Christ.

Tradition records that in the midsixties, during the reign of Emperor Nero, Paul was beheaded. He had previously written his epitaph of faith: "It is my eager expectation and hope that I shall not at all be ashamed, but that with full courage now as always Christ will be honored in my body, whether by life or by death. For to me to live is Christ, and to die is gain."

From *Man of His Time* to *Powerful Witness of the Faith*

Paul is known so well by his own revelation, but he is also known so little. It is easy to caricature him, drawing him out of proportion—a Calvinistic Paul with distancing rhetoric, a fanatical Paul, a controversial Paul.

In Lystra Barnabas was viewed as Jupiter and Paul as Mercury (because of his speaking or because he was small?). To the Corinthians he wrote that "his bodily presence was weak." A third century caricature drew him as small, with meeting eyebrows and large nose, bald, bow-legged, strongly built, full of grace. Raphael pictured him on Mars Hill in Athens as being of commanding presence.

He himself spoke of a physical problem, a "thorn in the flesh." We do not know what Paul referred to. Strong cases have been made for malaria, epilepsy, ophthamalia, melancholy, or poor speech, perhaps stuttering.

Whatever picture of Paul this creates, one impression comes through clearly. The primary reason for his great success at leading the church was not his looks, his compelling writing, or his powerful preaching; it was his openness, his vulnerability, his transparency, and his intensity. Some may see him as arrogant, yet that seeming arrogance is really transparency—a disarming honesty and openness that, at the same time, confesses his weakness and his powerful faith in the one who is the central focus of his life—Jesus Christ.

B. Gifts and Leadership

by Sherrill D. Hayes

If the statement "For me to live is Christ" is central to the personal commitment and character of Paul of Tarsus, then it is not difficult for us to understand his concern for and dedication to church planting and nurturing of the infant church. For Paul the church, the body of Christ, was the incarnation of Jesus Christ. The church for him was the body in which Christ dwells.

Writing to the church at Colossae, Paul spoke of the mystery: "Christ in you, the hope of glory" (Col. 1:27). This lofty view of the church is particularly interesting in light of the status of the church in his time. Paul, who could have chosen an independent route and established his own following, chose rather to become a part of the Christian community. It was infant, immature, filled with internal stress and lack of organization. Its leadership was "uneducated" and its membership was largely the poor, common people of the day. Yet Paul's desire to be associated with and a part of the Jerusalem church is clear.

Persons who today take their church loyalties and covenants lightly or who tend toward independent, individualistic approaches would not receive much support or enthusiasm from Paul. Confronted by Christ, prepared for service, Paul endured persecution for the church and persevered in building up the body of Christ.

Some thirty times in Paul's writings he refers to the need for the church to be "built up" or "editifed" in personal character, faith, and usefulness. He did not leave us wondering just how this could be done. It would happen as followers of Christ used the gifts given them by the Holy Spirit to equip the saints, for the work of ministry, for building up the body of Christ, until we all attain to the unity of the faith and of the knowledge

216

of the Son of God . . . to the measure of the stature of the fulness of Christ" (Eph. 4:12-13, RSV).

In his theology of spiritual gifts, Paul has left us with some important clues to understanding our own leadership potential and for developing leadership in the church. The experience of the writer in developing his own gifts and in enabling others to discover and use their gifts speaks to the value of Paul's theology in providing the church with leadership today.

Developing Leaders in the Church

Growing tired of ministerial studies that seemed too boring, too theoretical, too lengthy and too costly, and feeling eager to get on with winning the world to Christ, I dropped out of college after my junior year and accepted an assignment at what was my first pastorate. This was no superchurch, mind you—our average worship attendance that first year was eighteen persons.

There I was confronted quickly and dramatically with the need for developing leaders in the church. Now, some thirty-two years later, after pastoring a congregation that is considerably larger, I am more aware than ever that one of the pastor's central tasks is to develop the leadership of the church or to "equip the saints for ministry."

I can still hear the prayer of one of the dear sisters in my first pastorate. She prayed the same prayer every Wednesday night at prayer meeting: "Dear Lord, bless this little church, and bless this little service we're having tonight, and bless our little pastor; and Lord, please send us some leaders." Now, nothing would have pleased me more than to see a bus arrive loaded with song leaders, piano players, Sunday school teachers, church visitors, and van drivers; but I soon learned they just weren't going to move in from some superchurch. If we were going to have leaders, they were going to have to be "us."

217

Leadership Development Approaches

Through the years my approach to leadership development has been a pilgrimage with identifiable milestones. Early in my ministry I was trained in the use of leadership training courses. There were "First Series Courses" that required five one-hour sessions and then "Second Series Courses" that required five two-hour sessions or ten one-hour sessions. Then we in the church grew dissatisfied with the idea of *training* leaders and, feeling that it was better to develop them, we saw the creation of a wide variety of leadership development courses.

More recently the church has been influenced by a growing understanding of volunteerism and has taken some clues from the secular world in efforts to develop leadership in the church. One of the most helpful insights from volunteerism has been an increased understanding of the importance of supporting volunteers or leaders of the church in their ministry. We have come now to talk about the task of motivating, recruiting, training, developing, and supporting leaders in the church.

The earlier approaches to teacher/leader training served us well in their time, and although the concepts of volunteerism are somewhat shallow theologically, they have provided helpful insights for the church. Two influences, however, have been at work in more recent years that have the potential to alter dramatically and strengthen significantly our approach to leadership development.

Motivating the Laity for Ministry

1. The *first influence*, new understanding of lay ministry, has changed my attitude; the second influence, spiritual gifts theology, has changed my methodology. Along with many others I have been concerned about the ministry of the laity for some time.

My concerns were given a real sense of urgency during my doctoral studies on the campus of Drew University. I had been reading a book on lay ministry by Lindgren and Shawchuck, *Let My people Go.* One day while walking through the woods on campus I felt God speaking to me as clearly as I ever had: "Pastor, in the churches you have served you have kept my people in captivity. I have work for them to do. You must free them. You must release them for real ministry in my name." As I lived with this exhilarating experience the thought became clear to me that before persons could be equipped for ministry, they would have to be freed—released for ministry.

Much energy has been used by pastors struggling somehow to help laypersons become more dedicated, more committed, more willing to work in the church. Yet every once in a while one can see laypersons get really excited about what they are doing and work at it with a commitment that is challenging. It is evident that laypersons want to serve. They want to do something for Christ. They need the fulfillment of discipleship. The question is, "How can we motivate persons and effectively help them find their place of ministry in the body of Christ?"

2. The *second influence,* spiritual gifts theology, is helping me find some answers to this question. Actually it's beginning to turn the whole process of programming and staffing upside down. For years I have been made aware of the variety of ways to program for the ministries of the church. Here's how it usually works. The pastor and Board of Christian Education decide that the church should open a child-care center. The process then includes finding a person to be the director, finding teachers and a cook, and providing for janitorial service, aides, administrative board members, office help, and so on. We create a program and then go hunting for persons willing and able to staff it.

Spiritual gifts theology turns this upside down. The approach is to help persons discover those special abilities for ministry with which God has gifted them and then to create an opportunity and setting in which those gifts can be exercised for Christ. Here's how this can work.

Lois came to my office to talk with me about new ways God was leading in her life. She was a registered pediatric nurse working in the neonatal unit of the local hospital. Lois shared that she had decided to take an early retirement, but she felt God had something special for her to do. After some exploration of possibilities, we met with the Family Life Center Committee of the church. The church facilities were made available to Lois for the purpose of an infant care center. The city had numerous child care centers for older children, but only one that could serve young infants. Although every program of ministry has its share of management problems, our infant-care center, which had its beginnings in an idea about a person's leadership gifts, was a much more effective and successful effort than was our earlier child-care center.

Organizing for Leadership Development

In the local congregation we sought to discover how spiritual gifts theology could revitalize leadership development. We were guided by seven basic concepts in Paul's theology of spiritual gifts:

1. spiritual gifts are given to believers by the Holy Spirit (1 Cor. 12:8-10);

2. without exception, spiritual gifts are given to each believer (1 Cor. 12:7);

3. spiritual gifts are gifts of God's grace (Eph. 4:7);

4. the spirit gives many different gifts, providing for rich diversity of ministry in the church (Romans 12:6);

5. spiritual gifts are meant to be employed for the benefit of others (Eph. 4:11, 12);

6. the gifted persons are parts of the body of Christ and therefore individually members one of another (1 Cor. 12);

7. gifts must always be used in love (1 Cor. 13).

We offered workshops on "Discovering Your Gifts." We aimed at including every person in the congregation. Follow-up meetings, Bible studies, and task forces helped persons put their gifts to work. A listing was kept of gifts persons were exploring. This list was used carefully in recruitment of persons and developing leadership training. It was also used to begin planning a strategy for and designing ministries and programs.

The Apostle Paul's advice to Timothy is appropriate for all of us in the church: "Hence I remind you to rekindle the gift of God that is within you" (2 Tim. 1:6, RSV). Another translation has "awaken the gift within you." If we do, there will be a resurgence of leader effectiveness in the church.

How You Might Use This Book

1. After reading through the chapter about a particular leader, think about that person's leadership. What made that person such an effective and outstanding leader? What skills did the leader have, what could they see, hear, and do that others could not?

Now read through the following section "The Characteristics of an Effective Leader" and check the six or seven that best fit the person whose leadership you are considering.

What about those characteristics makes them so important to you?

How would you characterize the style of leadership of this biblical leader?

2. Now think about your own leadership. Remember specific instances when you were especially effective.

What made you effective? What about your leadership pleases you most? Why?

Compare the characteristics of your leadership with those of one or more of the biblical leaders.

Which of the biblical leaders in this book would you wish your leadership to be most like? Why?

What will you need to do to strengthen the weakest spots in your leadership?

What about your leadership disappoints and concerns you?

How will you go about working on the weak points in your leadership?

Identify the steps you will take to improve the effectiveness of your leadership?

How can I invest more time and energy into becoming more competent? What will I need to do to feel more adequate in my work and leadership?

What can I do to invest more time and energy into creatively developing the institutions I work with so they can be of greater service?

How can I more fully be in partnership in building up the church as body of Christ?

How can I invest more time on the personal disciplines of Bible study, prayer, and meditation?

What do I need to be doing to insure that others have opportunity to develop their leadership?

Am I too cautious in my leadership? Do I need to take more personal risks in exercising my leadership and in living out the values I believe to be vital and life-giving?

What actions do I need to consider for confronting and correcting the conditions of human oppression?

Do I know myself well enough that I am able to be so present with another person that he or she can feel free to be more fully and clearly himself or herself?

Do I have a sufficient number of close friends and peers with whom I can talk openly about personal needs and leadership concerns?

Do I know how to relax so I can get away from the concerns of my work and leadership?

Are my interpersonal skills sufficiently developed that I can communicate effectively with colleagues, group, and family members?

Can I face and accept my limitations and admit these to my colleagues?

Am I able to worship personally and corporately in way that enable me to be renewed and refreshed?

Am I enough in control of my time and my life that the results I desire can be realized?

Characteristics of an Effective Leader

—A trusted servant
—A caring listener
—Creative and imaginative
—Visionary and an enabler of visions in others
—A finder of new paths and ways
—Know what to say and how little or much to say
—A sense of perspective, able to step back and take the
  longer look

—Committed and persistent
—Assurance of God's call
—An encourager, enabler, mobilizer, and motivator
—Cares about causes and organizations
—Shares leadership with others
—Respects dignity and worth of all persons
—Patient and appreciative
—Able to manage and utilize conflict
—Sensitive to situational nature of leadership
—Able to hold on or let go and wise enough to know
   which is indicated
—Able to walk in the shoes of another
—Able to see beyond the obvious, to foresee the unfore-
   seeable
—Aware and perceptive, persuasive, and influential
—Good timing—able to do right thing at right time
—Able to establish rapport
—A team builder and participant—not a Lone Ranger
—Inner-directed
—Confident and hopeful, contented, and at peace
—A sense of justice and fairness
—Decisive, courageous, and able to stand alone when
   necessary
—A sense of history
—An international world view, a global outlook
—Able to discern good and best, evil and good
—Create climates of openness and caring where people
   can learn from each other
—An empowerer of others
—A leader and a manager recognizes that many are
   over-managed and underled

Donald A. Courtney, Leader

Donald Addison Courtney was a leader. He was centrally concerned with leadership in the church. It is therefore appropriate that this volume, written by his friends and associates, should concern itself with leadership in the church. Don had a vital relationship with Jesus Christ and felt drawn to his Lord and informed of Christ's way through the pages of the Bible, and so it is also appropriate that this volume look at leadership from a perspective of the Bible and particularly the people in it. Don was concerned to bring the viewpoints of various people to bear together on concerns, and it is appropriate therefore that this volume bring together a variety of views toward leadership from varying disciplines and ways of thinking but with a common dedication to servanthood.

As a Christian education leader himself, Don constantly faced in his ministry issues related to leadership. Here was one of the central concerns and problems of the local churches he was seeking to serve, early as a pastor and later as a national church executive. Where may we find leaders? How may we recruit them for service? How may we educate them? How may they develop and deepen their skills? The magazine he edited for many years was itself called *Christian Leadership*. Each year he wrote editorials in the field of leadership. The last class he taught at Anderson University was on administration and leadership. He wrote a book with Iris Ferren in administration, undergirded by a carefully wrought philosophy of leadership.

This future leader of the church was born in the western Pennsylvania town of Rochester on June 16, 1929, to Edwin and Thelma Courtney. His father, an aggressive and competitive man, was involved in the insurance and real estate business, and he dreamed that one of his sons would be a lawyer and the other a doctor.

By the time Don was in the fifth grade, he had developed his own lawncare business in the neighborhood. Later he and his brother Paul, who eventually did become an attorney, both worked for the local Hamilton Awning Company. In high school Don combined activity in football, baseball, and track with leadership in student government and being a good classroom student. He was in many ways the "All-American" high school boy.

As a senior he met, in student council, a freshman class representative named Nancy Lindahl, a charming blonde cheerleader. He walked "Petie" home from student council one afternoon and their friendship was under way.

Don went off to near-by Grove City College where he became a chemistry major on his way toward the medical career his parents had envisioned for him. Don played football, ran track, and kept in touch with Petie. Then he transferred to the University of Pittsburgh where he graduated in 1951.

Meanwhile Don and Petie were both attending the Methodist Church in Bridgeport. Here, while Don was a junior in college and Petie a senior in high school, they dedicated their lives to Christ. Jane Black, then a youth worker in that church, became very influential in their lives.

After high school Petie went to business college and then took a job at Westinghouse as the young pair looked toward marriage. The wedding took place in November, 1950.

By now, Don, the young Christian, was feeling increasingly concerned to enter the ministry of the church. His father was not pleased for Don to give up the dream of a medical career, but Don began looking around at various seminaries. He knew his dad was not going to be cooperative about helping him make that particular step. With that in mind Jane Black, who worked for the Arch Snyder automobile dealership, arranged for Don to borrow a car from her boss who told him about the big

228

annual gathering of the Church of God in Anderson, Indiana, known as the International Convention (Camp Meeting). Don decided to drive out for camp meeting and look over Anderson School of Theology.

In Anderson he visited with Dean Gene W. Newberry of the seminary and with Robert H. Reardon, president of Anderson College. Don became convinced that this would be the place for him to work at his seminary education. He returned to Beaver, and he and Petie quit their jobs. Don went back out to Anderson to look for a job and a place for them to live. He landed on East Fifth Street where Henry Leedom found Don one day with discouragement on his face, sitting on the suitcase, and not knowing quite which way to turn.

Mr. Leedom took Don in and in fact gave the young couple a place to stay during their first weeks in town. Don found a factory job at Delco Remy, and the Courtneys settled into their new routine. When daughter Becky was born in 1952, Jane Black came out from Beaver to help out. Don enjoyed his days in seminary and was particularly influenced by Dr. T. Franklin Miller, then executive secretary of the Board of Christian Education and a teacher of Christian Education at the school. Don became youth pastor at Noble Street Methodist Church, which also helped him sharpen his interest in the Christian Education field.

Upon graduation with his Master of Divinity degree in 1954, the Courtneys' eyes turned back to western Pennsylvania where Don accepted a call to become pastor at Vandergrift. They arrived there in time for first son Don to be born at Rochester, Pennsylvania, the same place where Papa Don had been born twenty-five years earlier. Don served the church but also began work on a master's degree in religious education, studying at Pitt with the renowned Dr. Lawrence Little. Second son David was born in 1956.

By now Anderson College was looking for a teacher in the Christian Education field. A letter from Dean Russell

Olt encouraged Don to launch full time into doctoral studies. He often preached in the surrounding area on weekends and taught classes at night at Pitt on the fellowship he had received. He completed his class work in 1958, returned to the campus at Anderson, and was granted his Ph.D. the next year. Along with his teaching he served as the part-time minister of education at North Anderson Church of God.

The orientation of this family to higher education is illustrated by the fact that for thirty-five straight years, with the exception of one year, someone in the Courtney family was studying in college. That extended from Don's graduation through Nancy's pursuit of a degree in education all the way through the graduation of the youngest Courtney daughter, Chrissie, from Anderson University.

The Courtney family kept growing, with the birth of Danny in 1958 and of Chrissie in 1964. Don himself transferred from undergraduate teaching on the Anderson campus to the seminary. After spending four years in the college and then four years in the seminary, he was called to the leadership of the staff of the Board of Christian Education of the Church of God in 1966.

For the next twenty years the Board was to provide the focal point of his ministry. It was a time of expanding service staff and ministry at the Board. Don was a strong proponent of the "family of agencies" concept and worked diligently with other general agencies of the church in joint planning, budget building, and common enterprises. He was an enthusiastic proponent of the Sunday school and spearheaded various programs to strengthen that educational arm of the church. In one of these he led the Board in a cooperative program with Warner Press and other agencies to launch new curriculum and related teacher and administrative programs in 1969. This same interest in the Sunday school led to establishment of a Sunday school program office and a new staff member during the closing years of his ministry.

Through all of this he was a family man with a strong

interest in all the activities of his wife and children. Camping and canoe trips took them all to the western United States. Generally they found a way to do some family vacationing in connection with the international youth conventions. The five children and Petie remember conventions in places like Boston, Dallas, Minneapolis, Seattle, San Diego, Miami, and Cincinnati and some of the travel adventures they experienced along with these.

Don was an ecumenical Christian and was widely concerned for the advancement of Christian Education and nurture not only in the Church of God but in Christendom in general and in settings around the world. For many years he served as chair of the Division of Christian Education of the National Council of Churches, a remarkable occurrence allowing him to influence that joint ministry of American churches even though the Church of God itself was not a member of the Council. He was recognized across the country as one of the preeminent spokespersons for religious education in the land. He was also concerned with Christian Education overseas and traveled widely serving the cause of educational ministry in many continents.

In his own home community, Don was active in his local church, and he was concerned with civic affairs through his membership in Rotary and his work with the Anderson School Board. He found time to do some counseling, and in this way reached out in a personal way into the homes of the city.

Don was also very active in the American Cancer Society. He came to realize personally the dread effects of this disease in 1968 when he underwent surgery three times within six weeks in a successful fight against melanoma. He spent most of his adult years working actively in the struggle against this illness, and then while still a vigorous fifty-six, the disease visited him again. After more than a year of valiant struggle, he died of a malignant brain tumor in 1986.

His ministry was cut short, but his contributions to

church, family, and community go on. Memories have not died. This book represents an expression of the memory with common concerns for leadership. The writers range from a college professor who was pointed toward ministry and educational ministry as a youth in Don's church at Vandergrift to colleagues in the teaching ministry while he was at Anderson University and the School of Theology, to staff members he recruited for the Board of Christian Education, fellow agency executives, friends in the ecumenical ministry, and to pastors and other leaders in Christian Education. The book calls for a new day in leadership in the church and builds on a base of influence coming directly from Donald Addison Courtney.

CONTRIBUTORS TO THIS VOLUME

John L. Albright. Pastor, First Church of God, Oak Lawn, Illionis.

Donald R. Brumfield, Professor of Specialized Ministries, Assistant Director of TELOS Degree Program, Mid-America Bible College, Oklahoma City, Oklahoma.

Joseph L. Cookston, Director of Sunday School Development, Board of Christian Education of the Church of God, Anderson, Indiana.

C. Richard Craghead, Jr. Associate Professor of Religion, Director of Master of Religion Program, Warner Pacific College, Portland, Oregon.

Edward L. Foggs. Executive Secretary, Executive Council of the Church of God, Anderson, Indiana.

Arlene S. Hall. Director of Center for Life-Long Learning, Anderson University, Anderson, Indiana.

Kenneth F. Hall. Professor of Christian Education; Chair, Department of Bible and Religion, Anderson University, Anderson, Indiana.

Sherrill D. Hayes. Executive Director, Board of Christian Education of the Church of God, Anderson, Indiana.

Betty Jo Hutchison. Former Chair, Board of Directors, Board of Christian Education of the Church of God; local Christian education leader, Columbus, Ohio.

Ima Jean Kidd. Director of Special Education and Outdoor Education, Education for Christian Life and Mission, New York, New York.

Juanita Evans Leonard. Associate Professor of Church and Society, School of Theology, Anderson University, Anderson, Indiana.

Alvin Lewis. Executive Director, National Association of the Church of God, Sharon, Pennsylvania.

Gertrude Little. Professor of Christian Education Emeritus, Anderson University, Anderson, Indiana.

Jim B. Luttrell. Minister of Education, North Avenue Church of God, Battle Creek, Michigan.

Arlo F. Newell. Editor in Chief, Warner Press, Inc., Anderson, Indiana.

Deanna G. Patrick. Editor of Children's Curriculum, Warner Press, Inc., Anderson, Indiana.

Thomas F. Pickens. Retired area and general agency executive and former missionary, Anderson, Indiana.

Kenneth G. Prunty. Associate Secretary and Director of Adult Ministry, Board of Christian Education of the Church of God, Anderson, Indiana.

Lynn B. Ridenhour. Director of Children's Ministry, Board of Christian Education of the Church of God, Anderson, Indiana.

Paul H. Rider. Pastor, Belvedere Chapel Church of God, Stone Mountain, Georgia.

Fredrick H. Shively. Professor of Bible and Religion; Director of Center for Ministry Education, Anderson University, Anderson, Indiana.

John E. Stanley. Associate Professor of Religion, Head of Department of Religion and Christian Ministries, Warner Pacific College, Portland, Oregon.

Marie Strong. Professor of Bible Emeritus, Anderson University, Pendleton, Indiana.